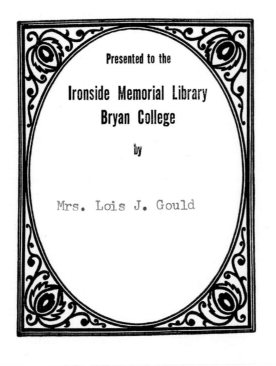

A Time to Dance

A Time to Dance

Symbolic Movement in Worship

MARGARET FISK TAYLOR

UNITED CHURCH PRESS

Philadelphia — Boston

This book is dedicated to those who have been active
in my choirs; and also to those who have not danced
but have given encouragement or have assisted in
music, costumes, lighting, transporting, and writing,
for surely, as they have given their time and their energy, they have been dancing deep within themselves.

Do you not know that your body is a temple of the Holy Spirit within you, which you have from God? . . . Glorify God in your body.

—1 Corinthians 6:19-20

I desire then that in every place the men should pray, lifting holy hands.

—1 Timothy 2:8

I appeal to you therefore, brethren, by the mercies of God, to present your bodies as a living sacrifice, holy and acceptable to God, which is your spiritual worship.

—Romans 12:1

For everything there is a season, . . .
  a time to mourn, and a time to dance.

—Ecclesiastes 3:1, 4

Contents

List of Illustrations

Introduction

For centuries the art of symbolic choral dance has been a neglected liturgical art.[1] During the twentieth century, however, it has grown creatively into an art that dramatizes the reality of faith. It is not an "art for art's sake" but a Christian art that can assist Christians in the worship of God and in the understanding of their fellowmen. It does not connect itself with any special group or style but blends into the life of the local church.

This art of symbolic dance has been known in a variety of ways through the years. The early Christian churches referred to the *chorós*—the Greek term for the choir that sang, spoke, and danced with the purpose of intensifying a mood. The churches in the middle ages and in the Renaissance period referred to circling carols, ring dances, and processional dances, which were performed by both the choirboys and the folk of the parish. And now in the twentieth century the church groups have a variety of titles—sacred dance, rhythmic choirs, symbolic movement choirs.

My first book, published in 1950, was entitled *The Art of the Rhythmic Choir;* its subtitle was "Worship Through Symbolic Movement." The term rhythmic choir was se-

1

lected because I felt that churches were used to singing choirs and speaking choirs and would accept rhythmic choirs. During the years since then churches all over the country and in every denomination have developed choirs that interpret through movement, choirs that have their distinct character in the title for their group and in their special emphases. During this time there have been many changes and today the name rhythmic choir seems too limited in meaning.

Since 1935, when I first became interested in this art, many titles have been used for choral movement groups in the churches—motion choir, rhythmic choir, sacred dance choir, liturgical dance choir, symbolic movement choir, worship choir, creative movement choir, dramatic movement choir, movement choir, interpreting choir, and dance choir. These choirs are all related but each has its own creative approach to movement and content as well as its own choice of title.

All the choirs include some of the essence of a general definition. They interpret through symbolic movement for the purpose of assisting in acts of worship. Their expressive movement patterns grow creatively out of inner feeling and insight and they are offered as an integral part of a devotional service. Their choreography and basic technique are often based on modern dance.

This book offers a glimpse into the use of the art of symbolic movement throughout the history of the Christian church and into its reawakened use in the Christian churches of the twentieth century. Also, practical suggestions are considered for starting and developing active groups in local churches. All the suggestions may be adapted, for there is no one way for movement choirs to be organized or developed. Each symbolic movement choir will have its own creative experiences in adapting to the life of its church and in opening new ways for the congregation to be involved in worship through this devotional art.

The participation in the art of symbolic movement by the folk of the church during past centuries points to the continued and essential value of active participation of youth and adults in the churches today. This brings a creative challenge to each church group.

Margaret Fisk Taylor

I

The
Art of Symbolic
Movement

There is an innate, creative impulse toward expressive movement in each of us human beings. Whether we have the opportunity or not to participate in a symbolic movement choir, we do have many chances to practice simple body-soul techniques: ways of relaxing, walking, and performing everyday activities—all connected with the discipline of awareness of spiritual power. We do not need to rush tensely to get things done so that we may then have a quiet time to meditate. We can learn to release our tensions, and thus gain increased energy for our tasks. In whatever we do we can practice physical discipline simultaneously with spiritual awareness.

5

INDIVIDUAL RESPONSE

To experience the art of symbolic movement is valuable for the individual of any age. Paul wrote in his letter to the people of Corinth: "Do you not know that your body is a temple of the Holy Spirit within you, which you have from God? . . . Glorify God in your body" (1 Cor. 6:19-20). The body can be trained to be an ally of the spirit, whether it is merely in learning how to release tensions or in creating symbolic motions. Glenn Clark included a daily "rhythms" period at the "Camps Farthest Out" for the relaxation of tensions as an aid to religious growth. In these religious camps adults explore ways of praying with their bodies as well as with their minds and souls.

At such a conference at the Isles of Shoals, New Hampshire, a minister's wife who had intended to skip the rhythms class joined the group on the lawn and observed how the leader explained the symbolic interpretation of the hymn "There's a Wideness in God's Mercy." [1] "The music started and I followed the movements," she said. "Then a miracle began to happen to me. The cold, hard shell of me which years of sermons, conferences, prayers, poems, and all the other phases of ordinary worship had left untouched, crumbled into dust. I looked at the vast blue sea as I stretched my arms to the side.

> There's a wideness in God's mercy,
> Like the wideness of the sea.

I sang softly and prayerfully as I began to realize the vast infinity of God's love."

6

THE ART OF SYMBOLIC MOVEMENT

MEANINGFUL FOR YOUTH

Symbolic dance has deep and valuable spiritual meaning for youth as well as for adults. A stronger base for loyalty to the church is established through consecrated participation than is possible solely through intellectual discussion of belief. Instead of "knowing about prayer" the young people can "experience praying."

They feel that they "belong" to the church. Instead of sitting in the pew and looking on, they have a place of significance to fill. The adult worshipers recognize them as instruments of expressive revelation. So, the young people experience the deep fellowship that comes with belonging to a group which is earnestly seeking the highest.

In adolescence, when there are many crises and frustrations, the relating of movement with great music releases tensions and fosters emotional stability. Similarly, when adolescents feel inadequate and resentful, release through dramatic movement comes to their aid. They may move to strong, discordant music as they act out their intense reactions to life. Creative expressions start with a sense of reality and gradually extend into a sense of relatedness.

7

Changes occur. The timid, tightly repressed individual learns wide, strong movements and relates his actions to others in the group. The hostile or resentful one finds an understanding acceptance of his genuine reactions and breaks from his isolation. Through mutual acceptance he and others enter into a new area of exploration. Slowly a new poise and assurance develops with a new freedom of the whole being—body, mind, and spirit.

Even as simple a matter as posture has psychological and spiritual implications. "Posture is dynamic, not static. It is a self-portrait of being. It is psychological as well as physiological. There is only one law of posture I have been able to discover—a perpendicular line connecting heaven and earth." [2] Creative dramatic movement offers assistance to individuals in finding themselves and in formulating their heaven-earth philosophy, for it helps them to stand straight in the midst of confusion and to move with resiliency when surrounded by pressures.

A balance between individual responsibility and group cooperation grows out of participation in a movement choir. Each member has a special place to fill and actions to perform to bring out the pattern and design of the religious interpretation. The practicing requires steady attendance and reliability. Group experience is a valuable means of educating for growth of character.

Whatever man enjoys, he progresses in and learns more readily. Religious growth becomes arrested for many people because they do not have stimulating avenues to spiritual understanding. Young people enjoy being in a movement choir partly because they do not feel self-conscious or conspicuous; they belong to a group that is like an a cappella choir in its sensitivity and responsibility. The balance of individual importance and group effort is a door to further creative achievement and group interaction. Such an art experience is not a pastime for youth, but basic training for Christian citizenship.

MEANINGFUL TO THE OBSERVER

A church congregation appreciates the consecrated contribution that a symbolic movement choir offers to worship. Religious interpretation is not an abstraction from life, but a vital involvement. The worshipers in the congregation are drawn unconsciously into identifying themselves with the interpreters. As Margaret Applegarth wrote spontaneously after observing a symbolic movement choir for the first time, she saw "true grace and self-forgetfulness" which had a re-creative effect on the worshipers "in lifting our spirits straight out of our bodies and then adjusting them back into us again as we too joined in longing for a similar grace and a similar reverence. I know that, as for myself, I felt an overwhelming joy!"

The inward kinesthetic response by members of the congregation means that even as they sit in pews as spectators they become vicarious participants with the symbolic movement choir. John Martin has described this interaction:

Since we respond muscularly to the strains in architectural masses and the attitudes of rocks, it is plain to be seen that we will respond even more vigorously to the action of a body like our own. We shall cease to be mere spectators and become participants in the movement that is presented to us, and though to all outward appearances we shall be sitting quietly, we shall nevertheless be dancing synthetically with all our musculature.[3]

A TIME TO DANCE

The universal language of symbolic movement is one of the rare religious arts which finds response in all who witness it, from the oldest to the youngest, the most spiritually sensitive to the seemingly insensitive, the most vigorous to those in need of health. The experience of religious insight that the congregation feels in the interpretations of a symbolic dance choir has a spiritual reality which draws everyone together into a spiritual union.

ESSENTIAL TODAY

Just as modern medical science recognizes the psychosomatic relationship of response in patients, so the church is becoming aware of the body-mind-soul relationship of response among the members of a congregation. The intellectual emphasis of the church has been necessary, but far too often it has deprived the ordinary man of direct religious experience. An art form may be a more direct channel for experience than intellectual discussion, although both may be interactively stimulating.

Beethoven had the ability to compose some of his greatest music after he was completely deaf, because he knew the harmony he was creating without the necessity of hearing it. For the average composer it is essential to hear the musical composition as it is being written. If Beethoven had not had a chance in his youth to hear tonal harmony, it is doubtful that he could have made his contribution in his later years. The church has been emphasizing complex theological theory, whereas the average person has not had the opportunity to experiment in basic areas of direct and total involvement in worship.

THE ART OF SYMBOLIC MOVEMENT

Movement symbols are elemental and universal as a means of communication between persons. They are more potent than symbols that are projected into other arts. Symbolic movements "speak" with direct and immediate communication.

The term symbol means basically "to bring together." The function of a symbol is (1) to bring together various relationships into a simple whole, (2) to make something more meaningful through this relationship, and (3) to gather significance for members of a group so that they understand what the symbol represents. Paul Tillich wrote that a symbol opens "levels of reality which otherwise are hidden and cannot be grasped in any other way." [4]

No area of communication is more dependent on symbolic expression than is religious experience.

Religious symbols are distinguished from others by the fact that they are a representation of that which is unconditionally beyond the conceptual sphere, they point to the ultimate reality implied in the religious act, to what concerns us ultimately.[5]

As members of a symbolic movement choir "point to" ultimate concerns, they feel involved in their symbolic actions.

The symbol expresses the goal which directs the course of action, but the goal is not separate from the steps by which it is reached. It is integral with the actions and with the quality of consciousness that permeates these acts. . . . It expresses itself, however, not in the fixed forms of dogma, but in the living fluidity of symbolic acts.[6]

What place, then, has the art of symbolic movement in worship today? A disciplined form of body-soul expression is one of the ways to lead the worshiper to a fuller religious experience. Evelyn Underhill, in her book *Worship,* has written:

Man . . . responds to him [God] best not by a simple movement of the mind, but by a rich and complex action, in which his whole nature is concerned. . . . He is framed for an existence which includes not only thought and speech, but gesture and manual action; and when he turns Godward, his life here will not be fully representative of his nature, nor will his act of worship be complete, unless all these forms of expression find a place in it. . . . Therefore those artistic creations, those musical sounds and rhythmic movements which so deeply satisfy the human need for expressive action, must all come in.[7]

Worship which has been centered in vocal prayer may use an art form that involves expression through a channel which does not use words alone. Allen Knight Chalmers, in his booklet *Adventures in Prayer,* asked: "Does God pay attention only to the movements of the lips and not to movements of the hands and body?"

Through the ages Christians have used the term body in a sacred way by calling the church "the body of Christ." Surely Christians of today can accept the body-spirit mixture of Christianity and encourage a religious art using a fusion of body, mind, and spirit. This art

is not new, but it is a deliberate attempt to develop strength, beauty, and power in the imaginative and the creative life of the participants and the audiences. Its immediate warrant lies in the need of our times for a spiritual ministry to the aesthetic and emotional life of our people.[8]

Even beyond the needs for the aesthetic and emotional life of church people is the need for active involvement. The Gutenberg era of verbalization brought on the inactive, argumentative, and secondary involvement of manipulating millions of words. We present-day Christians, according to Harvey Cox,[9] are now moving from written and spoken communication to visual imagery as the communication with more impact and acceptance. We are beginning to face the problem of communicating the gospel to the "postliterate man" who will be reached through direct and immediate experience.

Perhaps this swing of emphasis away from preponderance of verbalization is needed to bring balance to Christian worship. In *The Shape of the Liturgy*, a classic study of Christian ways of worship by Dom Gregory Dix, the early forms of faith in the apostolic age are described as, not something *spoken*, but something *done*. Symbolic movement choirs and sacred dance choirs—with the people of the local church participating—can assist in this art which communicates and involves the whole person in meaningful action.

2

Starting a Symbolic Movement Choir

A symbolic movement choir is not just another choir or an organization for youth to join as a social group. It is not a gimmick by which to interest youth in coming to church. A symbolic movement choir or a sacred dance choir is a serious and dedicated group.

Each member should be seeking to know what worship through symbolic movement is. The expression of faith through symbolic actions must be both simple and sincere. The movements must be so simple that those in the congregation can imagine themselves doing what the choir members are doing. If the action is complicated, the members of the movement choir may be concentrating so much on the complex sequence that they are not worshiping (just performing) and those in the congregation then become "observers of a spectacle," no longer worshipers. Empathy is the bond that unites the choir and the congregation and this comes through simplicity of movement and sincerity of meaning. This interrelation of simplicity and meaning was recognized by the sculptor Brancuşi, who said, "Simplicity is not the aim of art, but one arrives at simplicity in approaching the real meaning of things." So the sincerity of the work grows from the members of the choir taking time to examine their faith. Then simple movements may be discovered to project meaningfully what they believe.

There is a basic framework for developing the interpretation of a theme; choreographing follows a general pattern. The director should choose a theme that has motivation for movement, repeat the theme with variation; then develop it with contrasts or searchings and bring it to a climax of strength, intensity, or new insight. In other words, there should be a statement (in movement) of a central theme, a restatement (repetition with some variation or contrast), then an emerging second statement that relates to the original statement but leads into a new depth, new intensity or

emphasis for its climax. There should be no set vocabulary of movements hardened into technical sequences but a clear vocabulary of meaningful movements. These must be motivated into sequences that have dramatic power and that progress to a climax.

In his essay "The Conditions of Creativity," Jerome Bruner analyzes how creativity evolves from fresh combinatorial acts through "connecting diverse experiences and ideas by the mediation of symbol and metaphor and image." [1] Creative individuals in movement choirs may be disengaged from conventional patterns of modern dance as they try to evolve meaningful movements.

In the selection of music or reading for accompaniment, the music or reading should offer an opportunity for some development. Music that offers no dramatic development and readings that allow for no restatements must never be chosen. Some selections may need adaptations in order to be usable for the art of symbolic movement. Most hymns are a difficult medium because they cover a panoramic content of thoughts with no dynamic quality and the music is solid and steady with no climax. A hymn tune should be selected that has a refrain or offers some dramatic development and stanzas that unfold a theme with some motivation. An anthem, music without words, or original music to fit the theme development is best.

To have a composer work with the movement choir is a great help. Many musical compositions by Bach, Handel, and Mozart were created for special religious occasions. Certainly today there ought to be encouragement in churches for composers to use their gifts for occasional services in which creative movement is used.

17

The organist of a great city church should be capable of preparing fresh music of his own writing for services at Christmas, Lent, Easter, and other seasons . . . in which some of the great themes and experiences of the spiritual life might be set forth with moving power by the combination of all the arts.[2]

THE DIRECTOR OR LEADER

The director or leader of the symbolic movement choir is of key importance. While he needs to have creative ability and an understanding of movement and design, it is most important that he have a strong faith and an enjoyment of persons. Leadership calls for more than technical training of the body; it calls for a keen mind and spiritual awareness. Jacques Maritain stated in his book *Art and Scholasticism:* "If you want to produce Christian work, be a Christian, and try to make a work of beauty into which you have put your heart; do not adopt a Christian pose. . . . If the beauty of the work is Christian, it is . . . because Christ is present in the soul of the artist by love." [3]

The art of dramatic movement requires dedicated leadership—not to organize a performing dance group, but to explore creatively the field of worship through symbolic movement. Many movement choirs start in churches with leaders who have had very little dance training. But if these choirs are to grow, the leaders may need to seek assistance from a dance educator in order to gain new ideas for adaptation. The leader and members of the movement choir may explore modern dance as taught in college courses, studio classes, seminary summer courses, Sacred Dance Guild workshops and institutes, summer conferences on religious arts, and religious drama workshops. They should attend dance programs and services presented by other movement choirs in churches, observe religious dances on television, and expose themselves to contemporary arts in general. These fields have interrelating values in stimulating the probings into communication through movement. There are books on choreography and the basics of modern dance by Barbara Mettler, Doris Humphrey, Agnes De Mille, and others. Studying their emphases will help to keep the creative process free from encrustments of habitual gestures and designs.

Patricia Jewitt, one of the leaders in religious dance, who has taught at the annual Religious Drama Workshop sponsored by the National Council of Churches, stated:

> Out of a workshop can come not only a knowledge of the tools of dance but also a shared experience of "awareness," a deepening of one's own faith and commitment, and increased appreciation of other human individuals. . . . Throughout any religious dance workshop the importance of each individual should be stressed. Each body is the "temple of the Holy Spirit" and each is unique in its manner of glorifying God.[4]

There should be both exposure to professional dance and also freedom to select what is meaningful and what should

19

be simplified for a church group. Just as the director of a church's singing choir goes to see opera, but does not expect in his one rehearsal a week to turn his volunteer choir into a Sunday morning opera company; so the director of a symbolic movement choir appreciates the opportunity to attend a modern dance program, but does not expect in the one rehearsal a week to develop a theater-oriented dance group out of his worship-centered movement choir.

Philip Saunders wrote in his instructions for presenting "Christmas Canticle," which the Garrett Theological Seminary students had portrayed in creative movement:

> Many adaptations will be necessary, depending upon the sanctuary, talents of the voluntary participants, degree of acceptance of the arts by the worshipers and the degree of effort and practice. Please remember that this presentation was written for the sanctuary and to be used as a regular worship service, not as a subjective performance for the entertainment of the congregation! If one feels the compulsion to use it as a performance, please be advised to check with the agents of the nearest professional performers, hire them, and charge admission at the church door! Get the point? Prepare and present this with a worshipful attitude without concern for a top-drawer show.

THE MEMBERSHIP

A church youth or adult group should have open membership, with no skill requirements.

> Movement is a language which the ordinary person may use more easily than any other to express those feelings, ideas, and experiences which transcend words. . . . It [dance] is an art which the most awkward and clumsy, the least gifted and the most graceless can take up and make their own.[5]

An ideal choir may vary from eight to fifteen members. If more than fifteen wish to join, the director may have to arrange for two groups to meet at different times; or some people may have to be on a waiting list.

Boys or men may be hesitant about joining the group. The director might suggest that they join the choir on a trial basis. During this trial period they should be involved in strong masculine parts so that they will realize they are needed for balance and contrast in the dramatic movement. Many movement choirs include boys and men, especially in college-age groups.

REHEARSAL PERIODS

Regular weekly rehearsals should be held. An hour and a half to two hours is a good time span. Part of the rehearsal session should be devoted to body-training, technique, and exercising. Another part of the time should be used in creative work and improvising, and part of the time must be spent on developing and rehearsing specific works.

BASIC TECHNIQUES

Although some basic techniques may be suggested, in general, this creative, Christian art cannot be circumscribed by specific techniques. "It would be idle therefore to try to discover a technique, a style, a system of rules, or a method of work peculiar to Christian art," wrote Jacques Maritain. "An art germinating and developing amongst Christians admits of an infinite variety." [6]

Some general basic techniques may deal with walking, kneeling, use of hands, discipline of eyes, and movements of exaltation.

To walk smoothly, with chest and head up, face and hands relaxed, and the balance of weight slightly forward is a basic discipline of the whole body. Such a walk reveals assurance and serenity, and is meaningful in processionals and recessionals.

To kneel is a universal, symbolic act in all religions and offers a variety of meanings. It may express meditation, humility, contrition, sorrow, repentance, or the complete giving over of self. The corresponding variations in kneeling range from the high kneel of meditation with the head slightly bowed, to the lower body position depicting hu-

22

mility, contrition, and sorrow, to the restless agony of repentance, and down to the prostrate position.[7] In kneeling it is well to go down slowly with the back straight and vertical. The bowing of the head should follow, not precede, the bending of the knee. In rising from a kneeling position, the participant should feel the first muscular impulse start at the center of the lower back, then gradually cause the shoulders to straighten, and continue up the neck until the head is drawn up. Then with focal attention high, he is ready to rise from the knees vertically with arms projecting as the final thrust of the upward impulse.

There should be attention to simplicity in the use of the *hands,* partly because it brings a unity to the movements of the group and partly because it is needed to express a disciplined selflessness that points beyond the person. The fingers should be "extended without tension, very seldom curved sharply inward. The extension of the middle finger lengthens the hand as it moves through space, and does not swing the movement back in upon itself." [8] The aim of selflessness requires that the hand project expression through and beyond itself.

> It is its [the hand's] function to give completion to movement and gestures. . . . A powerful gesture with the body cannot fully convince unless the hand is in accord with it, nor can a subtle, restrained one be completely so without the hand in full consonance. . . . It can project movements seemingly to infinity.[9]

The *eyes* are as important as any other part of the body in communicating religious ideas. If the eyes of the participants are wandering, shifting, watching others—and thus indicating lack of total involvement in worship—the com-

23

munication through the movement choir will be distracting and fragmented, and the act of worship for those in the congregation will be confused and blocked. The members of the movement choir should practice the discipline of walking with the eyes held steady and with understanding of what the eyes communicate—in looking far off, or directly ahead, or down. Inversely, they can practice walking with eyes held on various focal points and then share with one another how they felt because of this discipline. For example, in the procession to Golgotha,[10] where would the eyes look if a member walked as Jesus walked? as Mary the Mother? Mary Magdalene? Simon the Cyrenian? other followers? The guards would present a chance for furtive and shifting eyes; they could be checking the people to detect the beginning of an uprising. Control of eyes is important.

There is rarely a worship experience that does not have a high moment; so, part of basic training is to learn to express *exaltation*. The uplifting movement of the body starts from the center, proceeding to a projected release of the chest; as the back arches, the head tilts upward with the eyes continuing the upward thrust. As the extension of the

arms through the fingertips is reached, the participant rises onto the ball of the forward foot.

"These are the rich resources of the body. . . . They must be disciplined and developed so that they can speak with truth and power. . . . Movement, in order to have power and eloquence, must spring from the organic center of the body." [11]

Seldom is a symbolic movement choir or sacred dance choir evenly balanced between technical excellence and spiritual depth; therefore even as the group works on improving technique, this must not appear as the most important effort. "An untrained group with something to say is preferable to a soulless, technically perfect group without a clear message. This is not meant to minimize the necessity for technique, but technique must not overshadow the real message." [12]

In order to explore creatively, the members of the group should feel that each one is accepted for his own individual way of moving and creating and that each one is an integral part of his group.

Betty Meredith-Jones describes an initial basic need:

If we are hoping to get people to become fully aware and understand the total wholeness we must help them back to a state of feeling in movement. . . . If we are going to do anything with this in relation to religion, we ourselves have to know what we feel. Once we do this—recapture a little of the feeling of who we are and how *we* express ourselves; only then are we going to be able to begin to relate to these vast areas which are ready for discovery. . . . We should get groups of people together able to feel that they can become a group, even if it takes a whole hour for them to do so in sitting, standing, or making simple movement related to life. There are simple forms such as the relationship of

25

ourselves to total space, what we see and feel in ritual, the most simple language of rising and sinking and the expression of natural attitudes. . . . We must first encourage inner quietness and sensitivity, an ability to work creatively on the spontaneity of the moment, and a willingness to wait for things to evolve when the time is right. From this starting place with the right leadership, we could begin to find the true meaning of religious dance.[13]

A hymn, text, piece of music, or dynamics problem may be selected for experimenting in many creative ways of interpretation. (An example of a "dynamics problem": Express hopelessness; then note where a growing edge of hope might start; recoil as if thwarted; reach out again; then see where the extending movement of hope may continue and arrive at some climax. A problem may be explored in groups of two or three persons who explore the dynamic interactions and changes that evolve—as in hostility that may change and evolve into gestures of understanding.) The director will want to be sure that everyone has some understanding of the meaning of the selected subject. It should be discussed to gain new insights. Then the choir can divide into small groups of three or four; these groups go off to different areas in the room to improvise and to work out related patterns of expressive movement.

After a period of fifteen minutes, the small groups gather and share their discoveries. The whole choir may "try out" some of the movements suggested. There should be evaluation of the creative works by bringing out what communicates well, what shows integrity of motivation, what needs further development.

Creating is a slow matter and should not be rushed or pressured, but should be allowed time to evolve. However, it must be admitted that creative ideas do emerge under pressure. A short creative period means that everyone works under pressure and only fragments of a total interpretation will be discovered, but even a short creative period is valuable in finding fresh and unusual ways to communicate.

DEVELOPING AND REHEARSING A SPECIFIC WORK

After the choreography for a specific selection has been worked out by the leader and the group, time must be spent in polishing the sequence of designs, in harmonizing the dramatic movements, in shaping the dynamic development. There must be continuous awareness of the content in the midst of its interpretation through movement. This period is an intense, involving time because it is the preparation for participation in a service of worship in the church. The selection should be rehearsed during a minimum of three weeks after the choreography has been worked out satisfactorily. The sequence of actions must sink deeply into the kinesthetic memory of each person so that his total being (mind and soul, as well as body) may be absorbed in what he is portraying.

27

A TIME TO DANCE

The persons are involved in all the dynamics of small group relationships and come to know the values of discipline, honest response, and group cooperation.

Individuals wrestle with Christian meanings and are stimulated to sharpen their ideas so that they can be accurately communicated to others.

Choir members experience firsthand the meaning of wholeness as body, mind, and spirit respond in harmony.

What happens to the individual in a choir is paramount. He must learn how the body moves, and how to say something with it. He must dedicate, train, and discipline the body to bring forth deep feelings and spiritual expressions. . . . Eventually he may develop a greater awareness of other's needs. He must desire to communicate with God sincerely and simply. He must also express God's promptings from within.[14]

ROBES

If there are no funds for robes, the girls can wear full dark skirts and plain white blouses. The boys can wear dark trousers and white shirts without ties. Sometimes the groups may wear choir gowns loaned by the singing choir.

If robes are to be made for the girls, a simple pattern may be used, based on the shape of an isosceles triangle, cutting the tip peak from the neck and allowing the width at the bottom of the skirt. The skirts should be the same length from the floor and should be above the ankle, possibly at calf length. A cord or sash may be worn at the waist. The sleeves may be dolman or batwing, having the wide area at the shoulder and narrowing at the wrist. Sometimes leotards are worn as a base under the sleeveless robe or as a base with a skirt plus a matching full collar, cowl, or V-shaped collar.

Jerkin tops may be made for the boys to wear over a shirt or sweater. Dark pants should be worn and the jerkin should be long enough to cover the thigh.

Deep colors are more effective than white. Gold, black, and green are possible for basic colors and then stoles or collars may be added for contrasts. Material should be opaque, washable, and dull-surfaced.

If there is danger of splinters or dirt, a rhythm sandal or soft ballet slipper may be needed. Usually members of a movement choir are barefooted. If this disturbs anyone, he should be reminded that Moses was told, "Put off your shoes, . . . for the place on which you are standing is holy ground" (Exod. 3:5).

3

Using
Movement in Festive
Services

When a symbolic movement choir is organized, the leader may discuss with the pastor the possibility of presenting symbolic interpretations in certain festive services during the church year.

PROCESSIONALS

Choir processionals are an accepted part of traditional worship. Each high season of the church year can have a processional of special symbolism for presentation at a regular worship service, a junior church service, or a vesper service. At Thanksgiving, César Franck's "Psalm 150" [1] can be both a choir processional and a dramatic presentation of harvest gifts. If the singing choir is in a loft at the back of the church or in stalls at the sides of a chancel, the attention can be centered on a motion choir patterned after the ancient Hebrew processions, with young people carrying gilded trumpets, harps, and timbrels, followed by a group carrying baskets of harvest gifts. As the last ones place their gifts at the altar, and as the singing choir reaches the four closing "alleluias," some members of the processional group come to the center, turn, and reach up, praising God "with the dance."

"Sing to the Lord of Harvest" by Jane M. Marshall is a processional that has occasional interludes. The total group, divided into units of threes (one person center and one on either side, with the center one starting a little ahead of the two side ones), makes a long processional down the aisle. During the first four singing sections, the units of three process with the alternation of the inner one and then the outer two. On the two remaining singing sections the group arrives in the chancel and there is a climax of dedication. This was presented at an Ecumenical Youth Choir Festival of massed singing choirs from many churches in Erie, Pennsylvania, in 1965. Junior high young people took part in this festive processional. The boys were the center single ones and their gestures were strong and definite; the girls were the outside pairs and their gestures were more lyrical.

A candlelight processional at Christmas and a palm processional on Palm Sunday are described in connection with Christmas and lenten programs in the following pages. These suggestions offer occasional variations for special Sundays and ways to introduce the value of symbolic movement within the framework of a traditional part of a worship service.

SPECIAL SERVICES ENRICHED

A symbolic movement choir brings added meaning to a service.

Christmas. Christmas services offer one of the most natural places for the contribution of a movement choir. Ever since Christmas programs progressed beyond the statue-like tableaux there has been experimentation in connection with the art of symbolic movement. It was in a Christmas pageant that I first attempted a small amount of movement simply by having angels, who stood in the background, lift their arms during the singing of the familiar lines of "Silent Night":

> With the angels let us sing
> Alleluia to our King!

People in the congregation sensed the aspiration of the "angels" who seemed drawn upward in adoration. The next year, after studying Renaissance paintings and sculpture, I created designs for parts of several carols where symbolic movement seemed a natural expression of reverence, dignity, and beauty.

If a Christmas program begins with a candlelight processional, "O Holy Night" by Adolphe Adam is a good selection. The members of the choir walk slowly toward the chancel, reaching it in time to kneel at

Fall on your knees,

and then in adoration they raise their candles evenly, with heads back and attention high above the tip of the candle flame during

Oh, hear the angel voices!

This design can be effective without candles; the choir members walk toward the chancel, holding their hands as "praying hands."

When symbolic movement is introduced for the first time, it is wise to present only one number and this should be slow, dignified, and reverent.

Carols were originally composed for movement and certain ones seem to be natural media for interpretation. The refrain of "Angels We Have Heard on High" suggests the possibility of variations in sweeping, wide turns during the "Gloria," ending with an upward reach, followed by kneeling, but still with a high focus during *in excelsis Deo.* "What Child Is This?" has a two-part pattern that lends itself, in the stanza, to simple progression or circling and, in the refrain, to joyous upward thrusts of exaltation. Another interpretation of this carol is possible using three persons. The first one interprets the first stanza and refrain. The second one interprets the second stanza and then the first two move symbolically together during the second refrain:

> Nails, spear shall pierce him through,
> The cross be borne for me, for you.

At the beginning of the third stanza, the third person comes forward and the other two who have been kneeling, rise and follow. They symbolize the three gift-bringers during the line

> So bring him incense, gold, and myrrh,

and continue the interpretation to its climax of joy and adoration.

The composer of the carol *In Dulci Jubilo* dreamed that he saw angels dancing in adoration as they sang this lilting melody, and upon waking, he wrote down the tune. In the

35

beautiful carols of the Renaissance period there is a real affinity for creative movement, which fits in well with Christmas programs.

For a more advanced group there are sections of Handel's *Messiah* that provide dramatic music for interpretation; starting with the passage "There were shepherds," continuing through the solo of the angel, also through "Fear not," and then culminating with the sudden appearance of the heavenly host "praising God and saying, 'Glory to God!'" This great chorus can be interpreted by an interweaving of designs to correspond to the interweaving of the voice parts. The accented "good wills" and the dramatic increasing and decreasing of intensity invite interpretive expression.

Benjamin Britten's *Ceremony of Carols* provides a variety of moods and tempos for interpreting choirs; "There Is No Rose" has been used more than the other carols.

Lent. To convey the lenten message, the church has turned to the arts of music, drama, and painting. The sister art of symbolic movement makes use of music and dramatic ideas to express the variety of moods connected with Lent and with Holy Week. Lent is a time of self-examination in the light of Christ. Whatever is penitential or is seeking humbly to relate Christians to their fellowmen in Christlike concern can be the subject matter of the music or writings to be interpreted by a symbolic movement choir. A spiritual, "Jesus Walked This Lonesome Valley," [2] may be the background for expressing the loneliness of Christ, followed by the realization that each person has to walk alone yet is not alone because of Christ (as in the second stanza, "We must walk this lonesome valley"). In the third

36

stanza ("You must go and stand your trial"), the facing by a Christian of his own trials—with the knowledge of Christ's power sustaining him and with the love of a concerned fellowship surrounding him—can be dramatically portrayed. Also, this spiritual may suggest Jesus' facing his trial on the night before his death.

The first Palm Sunday may be dramatized by a choir processional down the main aisle of the church. If palm branches or fronds are used, an added climax can be achieved by lifting the branches as each choir member reaches the chancel or during the singing of "hosannas."

Good Friday offers dramatic intensity and the stirring message of redemption. In the *Seven Last Words,* Theodore Dubois brings out the bitterness of the mob with the cries:

> He is death guilty! He is death guilty!
> Take him! Take him! Let us crucify him!

The addition of a dramatic movement choir of both men and women makes this part of the cantata more vivid by

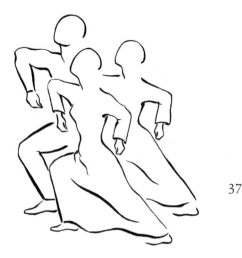

37

contributing a visual portrayal simultaneously with the auditory experience. With throbbing, angular movements the group presses forward. Skillful use of lighting which casts immense, menacing shadows projects a mood of imminent violence. As the mob moves about restlessly with sharp, stylized gestures, it expresses the callous words:

Be his blood on us and on our children!

Again it surges forward to the music of:

He is death guilty!

But as a soloist sings

Then they did crucify Jesus and the two thieves,

those in the mob crouch low and their shadows disappear. Gradually the single shadow of a man with outstretched arms emerges, high and lifted up. Soon after, two similar shadows appear on either side as the soloist continues:

One at his left, the other at his right.

But the restless group has subsided only temporarily. Now it rushes forward again with its repeated pattern of criminal intent. As the mob comes together with violent, outstretched hands, the words of Jesus are heard:

Father, Father, forgive them, for they
know not what they do.

Light from above floods over them during these words, and they sink down slowly with attention drawn to the light, even as they cringe before it in fear and agony. They are beginning to comprehend what they have done.

38

A simple but meaningful interpretation for the lenten season is "The Three Marys." The music background may be three stanzas of "When I Survey the Wondrous Cross" or "O Sacred Head, Now Wounded." The portrayal of the three Marys is based on John 19:25, which tells of the presence of three women at the foot of the cross—Mary, the mother of Jesus; Mary, the wife of Clopas; and Mary Magdalene. There was a dramatic presentation of the three Marys as early as the tenth century in the *Quem Quaeritus* in early liturgy. By the twelfth century this incident was interpreted symbolically with music, gestures, and speech in the *Planctus*.

The twentieth-century interpretation has a special depth and meaning of its own. The three Marys stand as a sculpture-like group in cloaks of gold, blue, and red. During the first stanza Mary Clopas, in gold, approaches the cross which is larger and higher than an altar cross. In sorrow, she kneels, rises, and with eyes upon the cross goes to the farther side and kneels with head slightly bowed. On the second stanza, Mary the Mother, in blue, comes forward. Her sorrow is expressed by more sweeping movements of grief. She kneels beside the cross on the nearer side. In the third stanza, Mary Magdalene, in red, comes to the center, lifts both arms, kneels, and with an opening movement, reveals her sorrow, leans back, and lowers her arms. It is Mary the Mother who rises first, then the others, and they turn as a group to leave. Their heads are up and they seem drawn together because of the sorrow which has given them a new spiritual bond with the Eternal.

One value of this symbolic portrayal is that it has its wider parallel in everyday living: the individual acceptance of tragedy, the dedication to deeper spiritual living, and the strengthened sense of fellowship with others who have also experienced "the dark night of the soul."

"Were You There When They Crucified My Lord?" and "He Never Said a Mumbling Word" are well-known spirituals that boys and men can portray with strong, repeated variations of the intense crushing agony of the crucifixion. Unless there is a large cross in the chancel, it is preferable for the group to consider that the cross is visible to them only in the upper corner of the chancel; then their moving toward the cross is diagonal. If a low central spotlight is used, it will cast enlarged shadows against the wall. The group should not have unison, stylized movements, but should move within the framework of the rhythm of the spiritual in their own intense reflection of the agony they are witnessing. When there is a solo part, one or two may rise to express the thought while the rest of the group cowers low with minimal movements. The agony must be felt with full intensity every moment by everyone through every part of his being.

Easter. It is Easter that calls for each art of the church to express the wonder and joy of the risen Christ. So the movement choir finds both the message and the music ready for joyous expression. The well-known hymn "Christ the Lord Is Risen Today, Alleluia" is easily interpreted in solo form as if the angel at the tomb is revealing the joy of the risen Christ. There are many Easter anthems with a variety of rhythms and emphases and with deep dramatic quality. A movement choir should become thoroughly familiar with an anthem and then gradually create its own symbolic patterns.

USING MOVEMENT IN FESTIVE SERVICES

"We will be merry far and wide, on this most holy
Eastertide, Alleluia," is an anthem originally written by
Praetorius of the seventeenth century and arranged by
Ralph E. Marryott. The interweaving of the voice parts
suggests that there could be a visualization with this pattern as its base and the costumes in four shades to correspond to the four voice parts of the anthem. This musical selection has many joyous "alleluias" which provide for
sweeping turns and upward thrusts of exaltation. In this
anthem there are sections that are reminiscent of sixteenth-
century carols, and other parts that suggest processionals;
thus it offers an unusual variety of rhythms in its expression
of Easter gladness.

Other joyous anthems are Gaul's "Russian Easter Alleluia," and Randall Thompson's "Alleluia." The hymn "Alleluia! The Strife Is O'er" by Palestrina (*ca.* 1551) offers
a slow rhythm in its expression of religious joy, and can be
as effective as more complicated compositions.

ACTS OF WORSHIP: SYMBOLIC DESIGNS

As the symbolic movement choir assists in the acts of worship, it should be considered part of a worship service, not
a side specialty. William Norman Guthrie, one of the earliest leaders in the use of the religious dance, wrote:

[The religious dance] must express meditation, prayer, and
praise so naturally as never to appear as a mere irrelevant . . .
illustration [which would] break up the continuity of worship.
. . . [It should] be done in the church . . . as an integral part
of some religious office—working not to a climax of surprise, but
to one, instead, of solemn and thrilling recognition of what is by
common tradition sacred.[3]

41

The processional can be used as a call to worship, the symbolic movement choir coming down the aisle portraying the congregation gathering and centering attention on the worship of God. Then comes the kneeling—symbolic of humility—and the upward reach—expressive of aspiration and seeking. Hymns with these possibilities for interpretation include: "Worship the Lord"; "Take My Life, and Let It Be"; "God Himself Is with Us"; "Rejoice, Ye Pure in Heart"; "Be Thou My Vision"; "God of Grace and God of Glory."

A processional with candles brings an added beauty to a vesper service. The carrying of candles symbolizes the bringing of the light of faith to a service of devotion. Gradually as the candles are placed in tall candelabra the chancel becomes radiant. If Bortnyanski's "Cherubim Song" is used, about two thirds of the music will cover the candle processional. There is a natural break in the anthem where the "Amen" appears; following that, the music increases in tempo and volume. Since the members of the interpreting choir will have placed the candles in the candelabra, they are free to express their devotion with upward reaches and to conclude in a mood of exaltation with whirling "alleluias."

The symbolic movement choir may be divided into two groups and offer alternating designs that join together at the climax of the devotional interpretation. The Bach chorale "Jesu, Joy of Man's Desiring" provides such a pattern for a divided group—one being the worshipers who move only during the singing sections, and the other being the circling choir that runs smoothly to the accompaniment between the vocal sections. During the fifth and sixth choral sections both groups merge into a unified group absorbed in dedication. The last two choral sections are used for the exit of the worshipers; the circling choir, which has moved during the instrumental sections, leaves the chancel during its final part.

Prayer may be expressed in symbolic movement. The Lord's Prayer is interpreted in many ways because of the creativity of each group and because of the special meanings chosen to be communicated. Music by Leroy Robertson is effective; so is the arrangement in *Rejoice: Music for the Worship of God in the Twentieth Century.*[4] Or the group may move to antiphonal readings—a phrase of the Lord's Prayer followed by an antiphonal reader amplifying the thought that is being expressed.[5] This prayer has been portrayed in a design facing the altar, in a circle,[6] and in V formation, and sometimes with a combination of these designs.

Dona Nobis Pacem, the sixteenth-century round with the prayer petition of "Give to us peace," is a favorite with youth groups. It has the simplicity of a single design learned by the group plus a seeming intricacy due to the division of the group into three sections that start their patterns at the successive intervals required in the singing of the round. This presents a round visualized. The first group of four is in blue as the ideal of heavenly peace; the second group of four is in gold, symbolizing the wisdom involved in the planning of peace; and the third group of four is in red, symbolizing the sacrifice needed in the bringing of peace. So these groups interweave in harmonious successions of outward, circling, and upward movements expressing their prayer for peace.

43

A TIME TO DANCE

At Lenoir Rhyne College in Hickory, North Carolina, a group of fourteen college men and women worked together to interpret the first setting of the liturgy in the new Lutheran hymnal. Then Pastor Keck, the college a cappella choir, and the symbolic movement choir presented their interpretation of the liturgy for the college students. All were worshiping—the participants and the congregation. The "drawing near," the petitions of the "Kyrie," the rejoicing of the "Gloria," the offertory processional, and the Lord's Prayer formed a continuous sequence of acts of worship.

The students had met each day for two weeks to study the implications of the liturgy and then to express them in meaningful action. They had chosen to renew the symbols through contemporary art. "For . . . it is through the actions and the implications of the liturgy that the church will seek to inform and purify the images and symbols and rhythms that constitute the imaginative style of its environing culture." [7]

Symbolic movement choirs have found new sources in liturgical music set in the contemporary idiom. *The Twen-*

tieth-Century Folk Mass by Geoffrey Beaumont has been interpreted in its entirety by some groups. *Rejoice* offers the liturgy in a setting of folk music with guitar accompaniment; it was composed by seminary students of the General Theological Seminary in New York City. Portions of it have been presented by symbolic movement choirs. *Appalachian Mass* by Eusebia Hunkins for solo voice and guitar has been interpreted by Roman Catholic and Protestant groups and contributes the variety of moods in the liturgy in a way that is stimulating for creative movement. Parts of *The Jazz Mass* by Joe Masters and of *Jazz Suite on the Mass Texts* by Lalo Schifrin are excellent in the dynamics of different moods for advanced groups to interpret. Father Norman J. O'Connor has written on the jacket of the recording of the latter work:

I believe prayers have been in need of a transfusion of life (more action) for some time. . . . If a man can't pray with all his talents involved, then his prayer will eventually end in dissatisfaction and annoyance. . . . But, one day, Schifrin's idea for the setting of the creed will become an act, a happening, in a church.

These suggestions may help those interested in symbolic dance to visualize some of the symbolic movement that reinforces the intellectual concept of prayer and worship. No movement choir should be hampered by imitation, but should be creative in working out its own interpretations. Its members will spend hours developing symbolic movements which fit the mood and the music. And when they present their interpretation in a service of worship, it will be their own act of consecration.

4

Dramatizing
Religious
Ideas

As drama is used in scripture, in music, and in preaching, so creative action may be used by the movement choir to dramatize religious truths and conflicts. But unless a church has come to understand the art of symbolic movement in its devotional emphasis, there may be some misunderstanding about the more dramatic presentations. The arts, however, are valuable in awakening people to dramatic conflicts that verbalization may have obscured. Worship is no longer considered a quiet, peaceful matter. In *Honest to God* there is an effort to make Christians face the world's confusions and hostilities as they worship.

47

The function of worship is to make us more sensitive . . . ; to focus, sharpen, and deepen our response to the world and to other people beyond the point of approximate concern . . . to that of ultimate concern; to purify and correct our loves in the light of Christ's love; and in him to find the grace and power to be the reconciled and reconciling community. Anything that achieves this or assists toward it is Christian worship.[1]

Certainly the dramatic movement choir can help in deepening the response to other people through dramatic portrayals that come from the Bible or that grow out of the conflicts and actions of present-day life.

MEN IN DRAMATIC MOVEMENT CHOIRS

Some movement choir numbers are effective with girls alone, but in dramatic portrayals there is need for the strength that men provide. The prodigal son, Job, and Boaz should be portrayed by men. In contemporary dramatic portrayals, men are needed to communicate the human involvement of both men and women in the agony and the energy of people. The men must use strong, direct, natural movement so that they project the reality of their convictions.

That men should appear in the dramatic portrayals of the early Christian church was even more to be expected than the participation of women. Most angels were represented as males both in the Scriptures and in the traditional art and early drama of the church. The nineteenth- and twentieth-century Christian church, which has been through a period of overfeminized art, could well afford to have male participation in its dramatic movement choirs.

SPECIAL EMPHASIS ON MOTIVATED MOVEMENT

Members of a dramatic movement choir must spend time in exploring movements that are motivated from a mood or problem. Doris Humphrey describes the way she offers a problem for students to work out creatively. "You are very disturbed by some emotional problem, but after wrestling with it briefly, you make a decision, either to face and conquer it, or to run away or otherwise conclude it." [2] So, first, each student expresses his emotional disturbance. "To understand this in a small assignment is to have a guide toward similar problems. . . . Deeply felt emotion always begins in the middle body, where the heart, the lungs, and the viscera respond immediately and first." [3] Other reactions follow—head, hands, legs, and other parts of the body—depending on the feeling.

The student should be asked to think specifically about his emotional state, not just indulge in vague agonizing. . . . Then we come to the decision. We must see it in unmistakable terms. . . . The psychologists tell us that strongly felt emotion has an instant reaction in the middle body.[4]

49

The student must be suffused with feeling and be totally involved, experiencing the "real roots of emotional behavior." He must be free to break from restraints and feel involved in a total intense way in hate, contempt, despair, jealousy, remorse, fear, confusion. Then, when the breakthrough of decision comes, this total involvement must be just as real and dynamic.

After such an encounter with a specific problem, the student should build on these sequences with some repetition, variation, and extension of the movements into a distortion that may communicate a symbolic significance. A slight stylization or abstraction lifts the action from pantomime into broader significance.

The essence of dramatic movement is *change* due to inner experience or in reaction to experience with others. Drama implies that something happens and brings about a change. The original intense mood must be clearly communicated, then the impact of other influences must be so obvious that the original mood is seen to change, like observing a person or persons crossing a bridge with leaps or with slow steps. Next, the impact of the new changed mood must be dynamically communicated. All three parts are equally important—the original mood, the bridge that motivates the change, the new dynamic mood; but the time spent on the three parts may vary. For instance, the bridge may be lengthened or be made brief; the new mood may affect a sequence of changes or the new mood may be just a suggestion of a new insight.

Dramatic portrayals usually involve individuals in relation to others[5]; so there must be training in the interrelations of the individuals. This requires a sensitivity to others[6]—a sensitivity that brings either identification or opposition, joining or avoiding, compassion or hostility, and many other reactions and combinations of reactions. The group will need to evaluate and discuss how well these motivations and reactions are communicated through dramatic movement.

Exploring his own reactions and motivations can assist an individual in developing mature insight. A teen-age group of 75 young people from 20 churches in the Los Angeles area have been meeting in the racially integrated Church of Christian Fellowship. Director Annette Bruce has described the work of the group as "a way for our youth to find themselves through a freedom of creative movements of dance. We feel we have found a way to help boys and girls become better adjusted persons through this creative approach which allows them to work out many of their innermost conflicts." Other leaders are Leonard Young, former Lester Horton dancer, and Van Whitfield, who has earned a master's degree in theater arts at U.C.L.A. and is currently a county probation department counselor. Here are adults in a church involved in assisting young people to mature through the creative work of dance-drama.

51

In both the Old and the New Testament there are dramatic stories that can be interpreted by movement choirs. A few that have been worked out for church presentation will be described.

"The Prodigal Son" [7] (as choreographed by the author and her group) begins after the prodigal has left his home. The prodigal rejoices in his freedom. But soon seven "vices" try to attract the prodigal who approaches one, then another, and finally pursues them as they dash off. The first part of Sibelius' *En Saga* was the musical background for this action. In the following scene, the prodigal's despair is symbolized by four "remorses" in shapeless robes and hoods of black jersey. To the accompaniment of the last half of Sibelius' "Swan of Tuonela," the remorses who have moved grotesquely to the relentless beat, gradually fade into the background. The prodigal son rises with an inner peace which has been reached through humility. He turns to go to his father as the music reinforces this mood of renewal.

The dramatic story of "Job: The Perennial Problem of Suffering" can be deeply moving. A strong, masculine lead is required for the part of Job. The messenger and the three friends should be men also, especially if the story is presented in modern dress. Because the problems of Job seem to be perennial, the group with which I worked in Hanover, New Hampshire, decided to present the story in contemporary style. William Blake's *Illustrations of the Book of Job* were used as guides for certain dramatic groupings. A Dartmouth student, John Lothrop, working closely with the group, created the musical accompaniment. Since the

approach was psycho-religious, neither Satan nor God had a visible part. The succession of scenes included the serenity of Job and his wife; Job's acceptance of the messenger's news of the loss of his possessions and his children; the bearing of physical suffering; and the three friends' arguments that Job must have sinned because a just God would not permit so much evil otherwise. The closing scene revealed the deeper awareness of God that Job achieved, going beyond moral equations to a new humility and release which lifted him into radiant light. All these inner conflicts and insights were expressed through the medium of dramatic movement, with Linda Lion (Smiley) as Job's wife and four Dartmouth College students as Job and his three friends.

53

The story of Ruth[8] is another biblical drama that lends itself to creative interpretation, especially enhanced by the dramatic music of César Franck's cantata *Ruth*. To hear this music is to feel the stirring possibilities it has for visual presentation. The following selections can be used for certain scenes: (1) the Farewell Chorus of Moabites, Trio of Naomi, Ruth, and Orpah; (2) Chorus of the Bethlehemites Welcoming Naomi and Ruth, Naomi's Tale of Woe; (3) the Chorus of the Reapers, the Meeting of Ruth and Boaz; and (4) the Prophetic Conclusion, the Union of Ruth and Boaz, and the Wedding Chorus.

DRAMATIC CONFLICTS (NON-BIBLICAL)

Dramatic portrayals do not need to be Bible-centered, but can deal with religious insights into conflicts of today.

"True Freedom," which follows, dramatizes the need to proclaim religious truth in meeting conflicts and problems. There are five episodes with narration preceding each section.

Episode 1: Humanity, in bondage, is searching for true freedom. The members of the humanity group (thirteen high school young people)—in shirts and robes of deep blue, maroon, green, and gold—come down the aisles with arms crossed shoulder-high to the accompaniment of a monotonous march. The narrator has just read:

> On and on comes humanity,
> Searching for true freedom;
> On and on comes humanity,
> Searching, but in bondage to itself.

Occasionally the music breaks into searching cadences and the choir members pause to reach high from side to side, with hands clasped tightly together. When all the members reach the chancel or the stage, their clasped hands come down on their necks like yokes that are too heavy to bear. So the group becomes crushed and slowly kneels.

Episode 2: The spokesmen for freedom are rejected. The narrator reads:

> Two arise as spokesmen for freedom.
> They proclaim:
> "Guard political freedom!
> Maintain freedom of the press!
> Encourage religious freedom!
> Protect freedom of speech!"
> But humanity continues its self-centered routine.
> When it does heed these appeals,
> Humanity turns upon these freedoms
> With mockery and antagonism.

The members of the group now rise and start to pace back and forth with complete indifference to one another and to two spokesmen who have ascended platforms at either side upstage. The two try to reach humanity to warn it to safeguard various freedoms. Some members of the group

55

stop for an instant, but then continue their self-centered pattern. When their attention is finally arrested, figures symbolic of various antagonistic viewpoints ascend the platform and crush the spokesmen down toward the center. They pause, converged upon the two spokesmen who are crouching as if to ward off the group.

Episode 3: Organization to gain security fails. The narrator continues:

> Two project their plans for freedom.
> They proclaim:
> "Organize to produce! Produce! Produce!
> Secure for yourselves freedom from want!
> Organize to defend! Defend! Defend!
> Insure for yourselves freedom from fear
> and freedom from oppression!"
> But humanity finds itself in bondage to
> mechanical organization.
> In its frenzy for total defense,
> It drives itself to chaos—
> Chaos and darkness.

These organizers begin to bring order out of the confusion by forming two rows of the humanity group who face each

other. The organizers set up a monotonous movement pattern of production, as if the groups were working mechanical presses. The left arm swings forward and up to a vertical position, then down, and immediately the right hand crosses to the left hand and back to the neighbor's left hand, as if there were a long assembly belt. The palms of the hands are parallel to the floor as if resting on an assembly line. Over and over the vertical and horizontal movements are repeated, as the two lines gradually pivot to form one single line. Suddenly, as the music changes from its monotonous beat to strident and piercing chords, alternate members of the group lunge forward violently, while the others push upward frantically. The fingers are extended intensely as the forward-lunging figures alternate to the right and to the left as if warding off threatening attack. The music increases in tempo and the group movements become rushed and chaotic, ending with humanity falling to the floor. A blackout increases the mood of despair, but a spotlight, centered on the cross, brings a radiant gleam.

Episode 4: Christ's revelation comes. The narrator continues:

> Out of the darkness shines the light of the cross,
> The cross of Christ.
> Hear his words for humanity
> That strives to find freedom
> Through ways that have no unity:
> "Seek first his kingdom
>   and his righteousness,
> And all these things shall be yours as well."
> "If you continue in my word, you are truly my
>   disciples, and you will know the truth,
>   and the truth will make you free."

A group of five—in gold robes—representing the revealers of Christianity, ascend the platform and kneel before the cross, then rise to express adoration as the music of inter-weaving "alleluias" is sung.

Episode 5: Christianity brings true freedom. The narrator reads the concluding lines:

> But Christianity is more than adoration.
> As Christ came to bring the abundant life to all,
> So Christianity reaches out to the fearful,
> To the disillusioned, and to the embittered,
> And points the way to the will of God,
> And the all-inclusive love of God.
> In joining to seek his will and to express his love,
> Humanity finds true freedom.

The revealers of Christianity go among those who symbolize fallen humanity; four of the fallen ones rise and rush fearfully away, but are drawn back as the revealers make wide movements pointing toward the cross. As they return, three others rise from their despair and bondage, which changes to release and vision as the revealers part the hands which have been clenched. As the revealers express spir-

itual joy the released ones echo their movements. Six others, who are resentful and defensive, move with sharp and bitter gestures. The palms of their hands in a vertical position express their rejection of any assistance, even though the revealers try to point them to a higher focus. As the resentful ones pause, two of the revealers express their awareness of God's all-inclusive love with wide, circling movements and turns. When they approach each of the resentful ones, with an upward surge of movement the defensive gestures are transformed by the lifting of the hands and the raising of the head.

All humanity has now caught the vision of true freedom based on personal commitment to Christ. The revealers merge into the humanity group and all are drawn into a wide outer circle and a peaked inner circle as the singing choir bursts into glorious "alleluias." After completing the circling designs of a related community, all gradually ascend the platform below the cross. On the closing "alleluia," as if from a deep inner impulse, they reach up, lost in a loyalty beyond themselves.

PSALMS

Psalms are filled with deep feelings of need, discourage-
ment, seeking, affirmation, rejoicing, and other emotions
that grow in intensity or are expressed in contrasts. Psalms
27,[9] 121, 130, and many others have been dramatized by
movement choirs. Often a speech choir accompanies the
movement choir, or the members of the movement choir
repeat the psalm as they move. The group should feel free
to repeat lines, to omit lines or phrases, and to choose its
translation in order to communicate the moods in the psalm
which has been selected.

Eili, Eili. Conflict, agony, and ultimate affirmation of
faith are briefly but dramatically portrayed to the music
of *Eili, Eili,* a Hassidic song from Poland (arranged by
Shallitt), with the words mainly from Psalm 22. Usually
this is interpreted by six men and eight women—the men
in deep-colored tunics and the women with long shawls
over deep-colored robes. Here is a blending of Hebrew
and Christian faith, for the psalm is Hebrew yet the first
line—"My God, my God, why hast thou forsaken me?"—
was uttered by Christ from the cross. At times it has been
interpreted by both Jewish and Christian young people in
the same group.

In *Eili, Eili* there is the blending of Hebrew agony,
Christian suffering, Polish despair, and present-day pain-
ful struggle—all with the search based on faith in the
midst of dark turmoil. In March, 1965, when students at
Ohio University gathered for a Concern for Human Rights
Rally, two college students of two races interpreted the
agony and the interrelation of the races. This was done to
the music of *Eili, Eili,* without the words. As the two stu-

60

dents moved with strong distortions apart and then with closely related searchings, the mass of individuals observing became united through the nonverbal but significant impact. It was a religious experience for all.

PARABLES

Even though a biblical parable may be chosen, it can be expanded into a dance-drama which presents the need of Christian outreach to the lonely ones of the world today. Patricia Jewitt has choreographed and presented "The Lost Sheep" at workshops and over television.

ACTS OF WORSHIP

The act of individual dedication. A first step in worship is individual dedication. Six members of the movement group come forward individually, in a scattered sequence, with various symbolic actions suggesting dedication of time, energy, will, and so on. Gradually they gather into a dedicated group before the altar. The organist may improvise or play a variation of "Take My Life, and Let It Be" as background for individual dedication.

The act of relating to others. As the organist starts to play Hindemith's "Sonata III" or César Franck's "Adagio," or as he improvises, the narrator reads:

> Wait not in mystic isolation your God to see.
> In every timid or discouraged soul,
> Where you sense your relatedness,
> God reveals his compassion anew.
>
> Reach out to the anguished,
> The tortured, and the hostile,
> Knowing salvation as a gift of God;
> Yes, knowing God's acceptance of each one.

At the start of this reading, the six individuals who have just dedicated themselves turn from the altar to be aware of others. For, at this moment, ten others rise from various places in the sanctuary and come to spaces on the chancel steps or on the floor level before the pulpit or lectern. They move in extremely distorted positions until they reach the spaces, then they hold their sculpture-like stances. They are twisted, crumpled, rigid, furtive—each one having selected his own way of distortion.

The six who had dedicated themselves now turn to assist by relating to others. They do not rush to those in agony; each one takes time to absorb deeply the intense agony of a certain other one. As each "assister" goes to his specific "other" who feels separated from God and from people, he starts by "feeling with" the sufferer, mirroring with his whole being the agonized position of the other person. He tries to communicate an individual-to-individual related-ness through understanding acceptance. The assister is at the same time aware of the possibility of the sufferer's po-

tentials. The assister sensitively relates to some gradual (or sudden) change of movement made by the other person, either because of fatigue from an intense, distorted position which demands some release or because of reaction to the assister's open acceptance of him. As one of the sufferers begins to sense acceptance, his movements change in quality and focus, for he is taking a first step in clarification. He may move toward the altar or he may become an assister, turning to some other person in a distorted posture. All this is close to improvisation each time, because the pairs or small groups become more aware and responsive. There are no exact movements for the purpose is response to others. Some of those in agony may resist any assistance, yet they will have known that there is concern and so one or two may remain hesitant or just begin to search. The assisters and sufferers have become a dynamic tapestry of interrelating before the altar and on the chancel steps.

The act of praise or prayer or dedication. The climax of the dedication that has turned into relatedness to others may be expressed through a gathering of the whole group to interpret the Lord's Prayer[10] or the Doxology, or to use a hymn as a rededication or affirmation. Certain stanzas of "God of Grace and God of Glory" may be used, with the congregation singing, to express a dramatic rededication to go out to face the times in which present-day man lives. Certain stanzas of "Rise Up, O Men of God!" may be used similarly with this closing stanza added:

> Go forth, O men of God!
> These times demand new power;
> With actions freed by faith that's strong,
> Go forth, confront this hour.

DRAMATIZING RELIGIOUS IDEAS

NEED FOR COMPOSERS

A dramatic movement choir needs the assistance of a composer, for it is difficult to find music that will fit into a dominant dramatic idea. "True Freedom," with its dramatic development, needed the contribution of William Yakovac, who was willing to experiment in the field of choreographic music and composed for and with the dramatic movement choir. For the dramatic portrayal of "Job" music was needed that would suit the plan for its development, and again a composer was found. At times the "Acts of Worship" (acts of dedication and relating) are presented with the organist improvising so that the dramatic movement choir has more freedom. To work with a composer is a privilege, and patience is required by the movement choir and the composer as they interrelate their arts into a creative whole.

5

The History of Symbolic Movement

The art of symbolic movement is neither a mushroom-type of growth that is springing up in many places, nor an art that is being grafted onto Christianity in the twentieth century. It has been a natural expression of man from his earliest days, throughout all civilizations, cultures, and religions, and is essential for man today.

The close connection between religious feeling and expressive movement has been coeval with the history of man. The use of expressive movement may well have been the first of the arts because it required no materials, but was a direct outlet for religious feeling. Among primitive peoples religion is a major part of life. Participation in group symbolic movements is so intertwined with religion that religious dances are considered indispensable and the natural way to express religious beliefs.

When I use the term dance, I mean the broad definition of moving in rhythm with a pattern of expression. In many primitive religions this term implied a pattern with gestures in which all the tribe could join—not a special form of exhibition or entertainment by a chosen few.

There has been considerable research in the dances of primitive peoples and in those of non-Christian cultures, and a wealth of material in this field is available at libraries. However, there has been little research on the history of this art in the Christian church, so this church history will be considered here.

The various references to the use of dance in the Old Testament may be grouped as "spontaneous" (arising out of a need to rejoice with the whole being) or as "folk" (joining of the people for traditional festivals or accepted ways of expressing praise). Prof. W. O. E. Oesterly gives a complete analysis of ancient Hebrew dancing in *The Sacred Dance*.[1] The Inbal dance group of Yemenites illustrates the folk quality of the ancient wedding dances and the spontaneous quality in their "Song of Deborah."

The spontaneity and the folk quality are obvious in these references:

Then Miriam, the prophetess, . . . took a timbrel in her hand; and all the women went out after her with timbrels and dancing (Exod. 15:20).

Is not this David, of whom they sing to one another in dances (1 Sam. 29:5)?

68

And David danced before the Lord with all his might (2 Sam. 6:14).

> Let them praise his name with dancing,
>> making melody to him with timbrel
>>> and lyre!
>>>> —Psalm 149:3
> Praise him with timbrel and dance.
>> —Psalm 150:4
> Thou hast turned for me my mourning
>> into dancing;
> thou hast loosed my sackcloth
> and girded me with gladness.
>> —Psalm 30:11
> A time to mourn, and a time to dance!
>> —Ecclesiastes 3:4

The Apocrypha also shows how the people joined together in dancing.

> Then all the women of Israel gathered to see her, . . . and some of them performed a dance for her . . . ; and she went before all the people in the dance, leading all the women, while all the men of Israel followed, . . . with songs on their lips (Jth. 15:12-13).

Christianity grew out of a strong Hebrew tradition which was cognizant of the natural, spontaneous, and accustomed way for people to express themselves.

GREEK INFLUENCES

In the early writings of the Christian church *chorós* was used repeatedly. This is a Greek term for "choral dances." Greek choral dancing had a special dignity and beauty because of its harmonious movements. The Greeks believed that the dance was the art which influenced the soul the most and that it provided the expressive way for that over-flow of awareness for which they had no words. The classic Greek dramas made use of choral dances to emphasize a mood or to reveal a vital meaning. So, in the writings of the early church—which were largely in Greek—*chorós* and the plural *choroi* were used. These terms have been translated as "dance," but it is important to remember that this choral movement involved folk participation in acts of worship.

THE FIRST FIVE CENTURIES

Although the New Testament has no direct reference to religious dance, there seems to have been no aversion in the early church to the use of the dance as an accepted expression of joy. A remark of Jesus, "We piped to you, and you did not dance" (Matt. 11:17), would indicate that Jesus was not against dancing, but recognized it as a normal means of expressing joy. Similarly, in his story about the rejoicing over the return of the prodigal son, he mentions that there was dancing (Luke 15:25).

Paul reminds the early Christians, in 1 Corinthians 6:19-20, that their *bodies are temples of the Holy Spirit* and that they should glorify God in their bodies as well as in their spirits. That manual action was a part of prayer expression is clearly expressed in Paul's letter to Timothy: "I desire then that in every place the men should pray, lifting holy hands" (1 Tim. 2:8). Paul respected the body as a channel for religious expression.

A circling dance of the disciples around Jesus is described in the apocryphal Acts of John written about A.D. 120. It is called the "Hymn of Jesus":

Now before he was taken by the lawless Jews, he gathered all of us together and said, "Before I am delivered up unto them let us sing a hymn to the Father, and so go forth to that which lieth before us." He bade us therefore make, as it were, a ring, holding one another's hands, and himself standing in the midst, he said, "Answer Amen unto me." He began then to sing a hymn and to say:

"Glory be to the Father."
And we, going about in a ring, answered him: *Amen.*
"Glory be to thee, Word: Glory be to thee, Grace. *Amen.*
I would be saved, and I would save. *Amen.*
Grace danceth. I would pipe; dance ye all. *Amen.*
I would mourn: lament ye all. *Amen.*
The number Eight singeth praise with us. *Amen.*
The number Twelve danceth on high. *Amen.*
The whole on high hath part in our dancing. *Amen.*
Who so danceth not, knoweth not what cometh to pass.
I would be united, and I would unite. *Amen.*
A door am I to thee that knockest at me. *Amen.*
Now answer thou unto my dancing.
Behold thyself in me who speak, and seeing what
    I do, keep silence about my mysteries.
Thou that dancest, perceive what I do, for there
    is this passion of the manhood, which I am
    about to suffer. For thou couldst not at
    all have understood what thou sufferest, if
    I had not been sent unto thee, as the Word
    of the Father. Thou that sawest what I
    suffer sawest me as suffering, and seeing it
    thou didst not abide but wert wholly moved.
    Who I am, thou shalt know when I depart.
    Learn thou to suffer, and thou shalt be able
    not to suffer. I would keep tune with holy
    souls. Do thou understand the whole, and having
    understood it, say: Glory be to the Father. *Amen.*"
Thus having danced with us the Lord went forth.

71

In *The Sacred Dance in Christendom,* G. R. S. Mead suggests that this hymn is an ancient mystery ritual of early Christendom. "It is . . . the sacred dance of the *unio mystica,* wherein the newborn disciple is united with the Master." [2] As indicated in the Acts of John, the group slowly circles round making a "mystic circle" and to each statement by Christ in the center there is the response "Amen." The "Hymn of Jesus" was not included in traditional Christian literature. However, it reveals that symbolic movement was employed in the second or third centuries.

The Christian Gnostics also had a labyrinthine design that interpreted the "Naassene Hymn" [3] in which the human soul is described as "wandering in the labyrinth of ills." The Savior descends bringing the Gnosis which frees the soul and leads her out of the labyrinth. In the well-known hymn "My Faith Looks Up to Thee," Ray Palmer envisions in a similar way the soul in a maze or labyrinth:

> When life's dark maze I tread,
> And griefs around me spread,
> Be thou my guide.

The *Didache* (a manual of church life and morals, possibly written as early as A.D. 150) mentions "The Cosmic Mystery of the Church," [4] which dealt with the mystery of the creation and involved a rhythmic interpretation of the sun, moon, stars, and planets.

In his *Quaestiones* Justin the Martyr, who was put to death in Rome about A.D. 165, says, "It is not for the little ones to sing alone, but rather together with musical instruments and dancing and rattles, just in the same way

as one enjoys songs and similar music in church." Perhaps this is a very early reference to children's choirs.

Various third-century church leaders wrote of the sacred *chorós* as a commendable form of expression for religious feeling. To Clement of Alexandria—as to any of his contemporaries versed in Greek philosophy—what was regular, rhythmical, harmonious, was also in some sense, divine. So he wrote of "those who have not yet been initiated in the mysteries or have no taste for dance and song" as being like that which is "dissonant, unrhythmical and material" and so "must still stand out from the divine *chorós*." [5] He describes the linking of song with festive movement as

the reverent festivals of the Word to the accompaniment of constantly repeated choral dancing. By righteousness man may take part in them. The song is a holy hymn to the king of all created things. . . . I become sanctified. . . . Thou also, if thou wishest, mayest let thyself be led. Then shalt thou dance in a ring, together with the angels, around him who is without beginning or end, the only true God, and God's Word is part of our song.[6]

Origen (*ca.* 225) mentions a hymn with the words "of the stars dancing in heaven for the salvation of the universe." [7] This hymn might have been connected with "The Cosmic Mystery of the Church" since it deals with the same subject. To Gregory Thaumaturgus (*ca.* 243) choral dance was a natural and spontaneous way of expressing religious joy. He declares, "The ring dance of the angels encircles him [Jesus Christ], singing his glory in heaven and proclaiming peace on earth." Later he writes, "Today Adam is resurrected and performs a ring dance with the angels, raised up to heaven." [8] He also expresses the joy of John the Baptist in this way: "Dance with me, Jordan River, and leap with me, and set thy waves in rhythm, for thy maker has come to thee in body." [9]

In Alexandria, the Meletians, followers of Bishop Meletius (*ca.* 326), had the custom of dancing while singing their hymns, clapping their hands, and striking numerous bells. To this day there are religious dances among the Coptic Christians in Egypt.

Men and women took part in circling and processional religious *choroi* in the fourth century. Eusebius (*ca.* 304)

74

states that Philo, in his essay *On the Contemplative Life* (*ca.* A.D. 26), describes a sacred all-night festival that was the same as that of the church in Eusebius' time.

> They first form two *choroi,* one of men and the other of women, and a leader . . . is chosen for each . . . ; they then chant hymns composed in God's honor in many meters and melodies, . . . sometimes one *chorós* beating the measure with their hands for the antiphonal chanting of the other, now dancing to the measure, . . . at times dancing in procession, at times set dances, and then circle dances right and left.[10]

According to Philo, this festal dance commemorated the triumphant dance of the Israelites after their miraculous passage through the Red Sea, "when both men and women, together . . . forming one *chorós* sang hymns of joyful thanks to God the Savior, Moses the prophet leading the men, and Miriam the prophetess, the women." Thus Eusebius quotes Philo to show how "dances and hymns taught them of God." [11]

David's dancing (2 Samuel 6:14) seemed to be a well-known justification for sacred dancing. Gregory of Nyssa (*ca.* 365) feels that David's dance signified "intense joy" and that he "by the rhythmic motions of his body thus showed in public his inner state of soul." [12]

Gregory of Nazianzus (*ca.* 369) describes the dance of David before the ark as "that swift course of revolution manifold ordained by God." "Dance to the honor of God" as an exercise "worthy of an emperor and of a Christian" is Gregory's advice to the emperor Julian, who had been reviving "the dissolute dances of Herodias and the pagans." Gregory urges, "Rather, perform the dances of King David before the ark; dance to the honor of God. Such exercises

75

of peace and piety are worthy of an emperor and a Christian." [13]

"The triumphant ring dance" is mentioned by Gregory of Nazianzus as a way to honor martyrs and to celebrate Easter.

> If we assemble to celebrate this festival in such a way that it shall be agreeable to Christ and at the same time honor the martyrs, then we must execute our triumphant ring dance. Great throngs of people must perform a ring dance for the martyrs in reverent honor of their precious blood.[14]

This ring dance or carol was participated in by large groups of people, so it must have been extremely simple and must have been for involvement rather than for observation.

Basil (*ca.* 369), who later became the bishop of Caesarea, refers to "those who now, together with the angels, dance the dance of the angels around God, just as in the flesh they performed a spiritual dance of life and, here on earth, a heavenly dance." [15] But at another time Basil condemns dances performed by women with frivolous and indecent movements. Against these the church always reacted strongly, whether they were danced in the church or at the graves of the martyrs.

Pantomimic dances and dramatic hymns were introduced into the liturgy and were received with enthusiasm. Arius had included a program of pantomimic dances commemorating the crucifixion in a liturgy called *Thalia*. Athanasius, his opponent, recognized the value of these additions and from the fourth century on there were more opportunities for dramatic movement in the liturgy.

There were also "customary dances" that the people knew and could participate in for special services for martyrs and saints. In a homily written at the close of the fourth century, on the anniversary of the martyrdom of Polyeucte, there are these words: "By what acts of grace can we return the love which he bore for God? If you so wish, then let us in his honor perform our customary dances." [16]

Ambrose (ca. 385) tried to clarify the values and dangers of the use of sacred dance. In referring to Luke 7:32 ("We piped to you, and you did not dance"), he says:

A simple speech, but by no means a simple mystery! And for that reason we must be careful not to be snared into a commonplace interpretation of this speech and suppose that we can abandon ourselves to the actor-like movements of indecent dances and to the romance of the stage; such things should be regarded as dissolute, even in youth. No, the dance should be conducted as did David when he danced before the ark of the Lord, for everything is right which springs from the fear of God. Let us not be ashamed of a show of reverence which will enrich the cult and deepen the adoration of Christ. For this reason the dance must in no wise be regarded as a mark of reverence for vanity and luxury, but as something which uplifts every living body instead of allowing the limbs to rest motionless upon the ground or the slow feet to become numb. . . . But thou, when thou comest to the font, do thou lift up thy hands. Thou art exhorted to show swifter feet in order that thou mayest thereby ascend to the everlasting life. This dance is an ally of faith and an honoring of grace. [17]

This last idea of coming to the font with "swifter feet" may suggest a patterned design as part of the preparation for baptism. In a contemporary hymn by Frances Havergal, "Take My Life, and Let It Be," there is the couplet:

> Take my feet, and let them be
> Swift and beautiful for thee.

Ambrose sought a means of spiritualizing the church dance and transforming it into a symbolic dance. In explaining Ezekiel 6:11 ("Thus says the Lord God: 'Clap your hands, and stamp your foot'") he writes, "Certainly there is a kind of handclapping for good deeds and endeavors. . . . These splendid gestures give a resounding echo. It is a noble dance in which the soul dances and the body is uplifted by good works." [18]

In referring to Luke 7:32, Ambrose writes:

The Lord bids us dance, not merely with the circling movements of the body, but with pious faith in him. . . . And just as he who dances with his body, rushing through the rotating movements of the limbs, acquires the right to a share in the round dance, in the same way he who dances the spiritual dance, always moving in the ecstasy of faith, acquires the right to dance in the ring of all creation.[19]

Here is a clear statement of the need to fuse the spiritual with the physical.

Chrysostom (ca. 386) noted the joy and the sense of unity expressed in sacred dance. He writes, "Of those in heaven and those upon the earth a unison is made—one general assembly, one single service of thanksgiving, one single transport of rejoicing, one joyous dance." [20]

In describing the celebration of the Whitsun festival, Chrysostom commends the Christians in a lecture, saying, "You danced those spiritual dances which are . . . most modest . . . ; you circled . . . and used musical instruments of the spirit, revealing your souls as do the musical instruments on which the Holy Spirit plays when he in-

78

stills his grace into your hearts." [21] Thus is noted the use
of dance and musical instruments at Whitsuntide.

"Dance to the glory of God" is Chrysostom's advice as
he holds before the Christians the example of David's
dances. He refers them to pictures which show David
"surrounded with his *choroi* of prophets who, in manifold
modes and figures, . . . [are] singing, playing [instru-
ments], and dancing to the glory of God." [22]

But he also warns them not to use "unseemly motions"
but to use decent gestures. Aware of pagan dancing, he
urges Christians to keep their dances sacred, reminding

79

them that God has not given them feet to use in shameful ways, but that they might "dance with the angels."

Augustine's warning (*ca.* 394) to keep the sacred dances disciplined is more severe. He is against "frivolous or unseemly" dances. However, he does not object to all dancing at sacred festivals. He can sense the harmony in the dances and the need for spiritual harmony in the participants. "For what is the meaning of dancing if it is not to harmonize the bodily movements with song. . . . Be ye harmonious yourselves in your habits as are the dancers in the movements of their limbs." [23]

Dancing in heaven was the occupation of the angels in the vision of Theodoret (*ca.* 430). When Theodoret wrote about the martyrs, he saw them in "their dance in the indestructible aeons." He urges his readers to follow their example that they might share in this dance, for they had been promised "the kingdom of the heavens, and life that hath no end, and light intelligible, and to dance in company with those free of all body." [24] Here certainly would be dance in its most spiritual form. Theodoret conceived of the sacred dance as a dance of the virtues in harmony with the powers above. What a change occurred in later centuries when the dance came to be considered the occupation of the vices in connection with the power of evil!

In Daniel 3, the dance seems to be associated with the salvation of those who are in the fiery furnace. Referring to the "Song of the Blessed Children," which describes the story in Daniel, Theodoret writes, "They summon to the dance both heaven and the waters above the heavens, and the powers that circle round the divine throne." [25] According to him, the flames of the burning fiery furnace

were turned miraculously into dew, "so that those blessed children danced the dance in their midst, and sang the hymn." [26]

During the first five centuries of the Christian era, the dance was recognized by the church as a natural way of expressing *joy*, a way of *salvation* and a way of *adoration*, as illustrated by the references to the dances of the holy ones, the martyrs, and the angels. The early Christians expressed in symbolic movement the deep joy that they felt in the coming of Christ, in the immortal life which the martyrs had earned, and in the close spiritual bond between heaven and earth. Their faith was not just an intellectual acceptance of certain beliefs; it was an experience of the abundant life and of spiritual joy. The early Christians entered into these simple dances as Christian folk, not as performers to be observed.

81

THE EARLY MIDDLE AGES (500-1100)

The period from the sixth to the twelfth century was marked by various crosscurrents. The church became more authoritarian and started to regulate all forms of liturgical activity. It began to legislate against some of the dances. Although there are occasional references to councils and papal authorities that opposed some religious dancing, it is difficult to know whether these disciplinary measures should be considered indicative of the total attitude or as valid judgment against some religious dances that had degenerated. Certainly the sacred dance was a form of religious expression in which the people participated. During this period, when the general culture was not stimulating, the church preserved and fostered the religious arts. It was at this time that the mass developed with its definite, prescribed, symbolic movements to the accompaniment of Gregorian chants.

The Alexandrian monk, Cosmas (*ca.* 550) in his painting "The Cosmos" not only depicts his idea of the universe with the sun, moon, and stars about the earth, but also suggests rhythmic patterns in the circling positions of the angels who held the stars and the two angels within the circle who carried the sun and moon around the earth. It may be that his painting of angels in symbolic movement had a relation to the dance of the cosmic mystery of creation mentioned in the *Didache*.

In a Gallican sacramentary of the seventh century this eucharistic prayer is included: "We beseech thee, almighty Father, eternal God, deliver us from all temptation, give us help in every conflict. . . . Grant that we may worship thee with a pure heart; let us dance before thee with a clean conscience; let us serve thee with all our strength." [27] Here was a combination of worship, dance, and serving.

It was customary to celebrate festivals and saints' days with some form of dancing. On the vigil of a saint's day, or a day of prayer, silence, and penance, of course dancing was not suitable to the penitential mood. So the edict of 539 by the Council of Toledo forbidding dancing in the churches during the vigil of saints' days was justifiable.

In the following century, the Council of Toledo suggested that Isidore, the archbishop of Seville, present a ritual that would be rich in sacred choreography. This ritual became incorporated into a mass known as *Mozarabe*. It was used in the seven churches of Toledo and is still celebrated today in the cathedral of Seville.

This *Mozarabe* with the dances of *los mozos de coro* (choristers) became known and authorized as the mass which included the dances of *los seises* according to a bull of Pope Eugenius IV in 1439. At that time *los seises* (originally six choirboys) danced before the ark on the altar and were "dressed as angels." The costume was composed of short, wide britches of Moorish cut; a short, sleeveless mantle; a tight-fitting jacket; wreaths of intertwined flowers worn on the bare head; and gilded wings affixed to the shoulders. Thus the dancing choristers really represented the angels in heaven who had descended to the church choir in order to continue there the dance of the blessed in paradise—quite similar to writings of Clement of Alexandria in A.D. 195. Later, in the Renaissance, the costume of a page was adopted and this is the costume still worn today. The choirboys wear red coats, short yellow breeches, red stockings, and hats with plumes.

83

A TIME TO DANCE

Los seises had a dramatic time at the end of the seventeenth century when the archbishop of Seville forbade the performance of their dance. Amazed at this ruling, the people of Seville collected enough money to send *los seises* (no longer six, but ten choristers now) all the way to Rome, where they performed their dances before the pope with singing and the clicking of castanets. It is reported that the pope said, "I see nothing in this children's dance which is offensive to God. Let them continue to dance before the high altar." And they have continued to do so!

Three times a year *los seises* dance—Shrove Tuesday, the Feast of Corpus Christi, and the Feast of the Immaculate Conception. In the dance of the *Immaculata, los seises* form two parallel lines of five. In the dance of the Corpus Christi festival *los seises* form the design of St. Andrew's cross while two choristers move in a narrow circle around the center of the cross.

One of their songs, noted in 1690, includes these lines:

> (*Standing still*)
> We believe in the bread of life
> From Christ to our overflowing joy;
> By our dance we supplicate him,
> As once the Baptist supplicated.
>
> (*Dancing during refrain*)
> Therefore by this dance
> We strengthen our firm faith,
> All to the sounds of music.[28]

Here is an example of the possible original use of the term stanza as the part of a song when all "stand" still in contrast to the refrain when there might be dancing.

84

The *baile de los seises* is described by Lagergren, who attended the mass in Seville in 1878.

Ten choristers [entered], dressed magnificently as pages of the seventeenth century. Standing before the high altar, first they dropped on their knees, then they rose and sang a curious melodious song; then they put on hats, divided into two groups, and stepped backward and forward, making figures and singing, sometimes accompanying themselves with castanets. "The dance . . . lasted about a quarter of an hour and made a very remarkable spectacle. The deep reverence of the spectators emphasized the strangeness of the performance." [29]

Recent visitors to Seville have observed the dances and recorded that part of the mass. This sacred dance has existed from the seventh century into the twentieth century!

Sacred dances continued to spread throughout Europe during the eighth and ninth centuries, but there were efforts to restrain degenerate forms that were appearing.

Dancing was a customary accompaniment to the processionals in which relics of saints or martyrs were carried, and it was part of the church festivals.

The word procession means a moving chorus advancing in harmony and with a sort of cadence through the various parts of the church. The processions passing through the choir and aisles . . . do so to measured movements prescribed in the ritual, . . . representing by their symbolic movements and figures holy and mystic dances.

This is recorded in the *Dictionnaire de plain-chant* (Paris, 1860).

In a liturgy of a Paris church, used about 900, a rubric reads: "Here the canon shall dance at the first psalm." This might have involved some symbolic movements and

gestures by the canon alone, or it may have pointed to a custom of the canon leading the choirboys in a circling design during the chanting of the psalms.

The Flagellants appeared in northern Italy in the eleventh century and spread to Germany and later to Spain and England. People of all classes and ages formed long processions which were headed by priests carrying crosses and banners. They walked through the streets in double file reciting prayers and drawing blood from their bodies by whipping themselves and each other with leather thongs. These exhibitions, symbolic of repentance, were suppressed somewhat, but have reappeared occasionally throughout the centuries, in various countries, including Mexico and the United States.

LATER MEDIEVAL PERIOD (1100-1400)

The later medieval period was an age of dramatic and emotional expression. The church, which had denounced the degenerate secular, theatrical productions, decided to create its own dramatic portrayals. It made a definite effort to arouse public interest in the service of the church by introducing more choral songs, picturesque processionals, and even ceremonial dances performed in the choir area.

There are various references to hymns that mention the dance as an accepted liturgical art form. In the tenth-century hymnary of the monastery of Moissac there is a hymn for morning mass during the Easter festivals:

> His [Christ's] life, his speech and miracles,
> His wondrous death prove it.
> The congregation adorns the sanctity;
> Come and behold the host of ring dances! [30]

Another church hymn sung during the Easter celebration is recorded:

> The salvation of the earth is at hand,
> Ye mortals; clap your hands,
> Ye who are saved, sing
> Your songs of triumph!
> Sing and dance to music (*tripudiantes*)
> And with honest mind
> Before the Lord of the heavens. [31]

This hymn includes references to the clapping of hands, singing, dancing, and even the activity of clear thinking!

During the eleventh century, the following hymn was sung on the birthday of Mary:

A TIME TO DANCE

Now clap in applause,
Ye men and women!
Tune up in harmony
Beautiful communal songs
And dance ring dances
In holy Mary's honor! [32]

Men and women—the folk of the parish—were active participants in the worship services.

The *Planctus*[33] appears as part of the mass early in the twelfth century. This is a religious play concerned with the sorrows of the three Marys. The actions to accompany the lines and musical score are specified by interlinear indications in red, or "rubrics":

Magdalene: O brothers!
             (*Turns to the people with arms held out.*)
             Where is my hope?
             (*Beats her breast.*)
             Where is my consolation?
             (*Raises her hands.*)
             Where is my whole salvation?
             (*Inclines her head, casts herself at Christ's feet.*)
             O Master mine?

Mother: O sorrow!
             Deep sorrow!
             Why, why indeed,
             (*Points to Christ with open hands.*)
             Dear Son, hangest thou thus,
             Thou who art life
             (*Beats her breast.*)
             And has forever been?

The third Mary follows with similar lines and actions. Later, Mary the Mother and Magdalene speak together.

88

The actors were clergy, holy sisters, or choirboys. The play was more often chanted to music than spoken. Here in an early form is the interrelation of gesture, music, verse, and meaning.

Mystery and miracle plays began to take form at this time. Sometimes they were presented in the *ballatoria* (dancing pavement) which was a space in the front of the church or at the west door, where awnings were hung. At other times they were transported and presented on wagon-stages. In France, England, and Germany there was a thriving interest in these plays, which included, besides the dramatic action, the dancing of the follies, devils, and Salome. The follies, which represented the vices, tried to attract people in the audience; the devil, as the leading dancer, with his troupe of assisting devils, enjoyed scaring them; and the acrobatic dancing of Salome entertained them. On the porch at Rouen there is a bas-relief of Salome in an acrobatic dance position. It is evident that the dancing connected with these religious dramatizations was mainly theatrical and not devotional.

Monastic orders, during the twelfth and thirteenth centuries, seemed to find the dance of religious value when used in their disciplined groups. It was the custom of the monks of the Cistercian Order to dance and pray for the salvation of the universe. The Franciscans sang and danced and called themselves the singing servants of Christ. Fra Jacapone da Todi (*ca.* 1270), a Franciscan monk, writes, "Oh, that each one who loves the Lord would join in the dance, singing of his devotion." [34] Friar Marti of Alicante found time to write a treatise on dancing, even during the period of the Inquisition. The nuns of Villaceaux cele-

brated the feasts of the Holy Innocents and Mary Magdalene with appropriate dances.

Bonaventura (*ca.* 1260) is aware of this parallel when
he writes that in the joys of paradise there will be endless
circling in rhythmic revolutions with the heavenly spheres
as the redeemed sing ceaseless songs of praise. "Blessed in
soothe is that dance (*chorea*) whose company is infinity,
whose circling is eternity, whose song is bliss." [35]

As late as the twelfth century, in the writings of the her-
mit Honorius, there is reference to a ritual dance similar to
the one mentioned in the second-century *Didache* as "The
Cosmic Mystery of the Church":

> In their ring dances they thought of the rotation of the firma-
> ment; in the clasping of their hands the union of the elements; in
> the sounds of song the harmony of the planets; in the gestures of
> the body the movements of the celestial bodies; in the clapping of
> the hands and the stamping of feet the sound of thunder; some-
> thing which the faithful imitate, converting all to the true service
> of God.[36]

Four kinds of choral dances (*tripudia*) are mentioned
by John Beleth, who lived in the twelfth century and was
rector of the University of Paris. The dances were customary for certain church festivals: the deacons' festival dance

on St. Stephen's Day, the priests' festival dance on St. John's Day, the choirboys' (later, the "children's") festival dance on Holy Innocents' Day (December 28) and the subdeacons' festival dance on the Feast of the Circumcision or of the Epiphany.

The children's festival, or the festival of the choristers, included dancing at divine service and at the celebration of the mass. In 1327 the church at Puy had a procession in which the choristers were to dance with great vigor (like King David's dancing) and then at the end of the mass the choristers were instructed to dance even more vigorously —*tripudiant fortiter.*

An English statute (end of the twelfth century) says, "It is the duty of the priest on Innocents' Day, when food has been eaten, to conduct his boys, dancing and carrying candles, to their quarters." [37] Evidently the children were given freedom for vigorous activity as choristers.

The well-known legend of the Juggler of Notre Dame was written down about 1286. It tells of a juggler who was admitted to a monastery but was unable to read the prayers. One day when he was alone in the chapel he sought to serve the virgin Mary by dancing. So, it is said, he danced to the right and to the left, hopped and glided. He begged Mary not to scorn his efforts but to accept them. Then he danced until he was exhausted and lay unconscious. One of the brothers had informed the abbot about this practice of the juggler-brother, so one day the brothers watched unnoticed. When they saw him lying on the ground exhausted at the end of his vigorous dancing, they witnessed Mary bending down to give him solace and blessing him with the sign of the cross. The abbot then assured

91

the juggler that he could serve God and the virgin Mary by his dancing.

This legend has been danced many times since the thirteenth century. An effective presentation was Conna Bell Shaw's dancing of "The Juggler" on the plaza in front of the chapel at Oberlin College, Oberlin, Ohio, in 1929. The modern dance groups assisted as villagers. More recently, Gus Solomons, Jr., danced "The Juggler of Notre Dame" on a 1964 program of the television series "Lamp unto My Feet."

Church labyrinthine dances seem to date from the eleventh century, although there is the earlier reference in the "Naassene Hymn" of the second century, with the line: "Wandering in the labyrinth of ills." In the cathedral at Chartres (*ca.* 1200) there was constructed in the floor a maze (or labyrinth) which was forty feet across. "Labyrinths were not uncommon . . . in medieval, and perhaps more ancient, churches. . . . Pilgrims to Chartres still practice the devotion of the rosary on the labyrinth." [38]

Geometrical figures composed of various pieces of colored marble and so disposed as to form labyrinths were frequently found in the pavements of French [and Spanish] cathedrals. . . . Certain prayers and devotions doubtless accompanied the perambulation of their intricate mazes. [39]

Often the people held hands as they wound around into and out of the maze.

The model of so many labyrinths in Christian churches was the Cretan labyrinth. The Minotaur became identified with Satan and Theseus became identified with Christ, who descended into the underworld, overcame Satan, and

emerged victorious, together with those who were saved.
The leader guided men and women holding each other
by the hand, following the bends of the labyrinth into the
center and then out to the release of salvation.

The following inscription is carved on a stone from a
labyrinth, preserved in the Lyons museum: "Look upon
this mirror and behold in it thine own mortality! . . .
Beg and pray to Christ that thy life may be lived in Christ,
that by the Easter festival thou mayest be awakened and
come out of the labyrinth." This suggests the eventual
exit and escape from death for followers of Christ. It was
a symbolic design which the people could follow with ease
and with meaning.

93

The symbolism of Christ "leading out" the people in
an Easter ceremony is illustrated in the account of the
processional dance in Hildesheim in 1478:

> Thereafter comes the solemn procession in memory of the pro-
> cession which Christ . . . solemnized when he returned from
> the underworld, leading out those he had delivered into the para-
> dise of ecstasy, dancing and hopping. He introduces both music
> and dance in consideration of the liberation of so many souls. He
> sings to them a song which none should utter except to God's im-
> mortal Son after his wondrous triumph. And we all, happy and
> adorned with spiritual perfection, follow our highest master, who
> himself leads the solemn ring dance.[40]

The contrast in the actions is worth noting: A *stanza* is
sung by a member of the clergy to the people as they *stand*
still; this is followed by the group's participating in the
"solemn ring dance." At the conclusion of the mass there
are these lines:

> O gracious Lord Sabaoth, . . .
> Lead us on in Easter dance;
> There we shall find our joy.[41]

The hymn writers of the fourteenth century made numerous references to ring dances and processional dances.
In Germany in the fourteenth century a monk composed
several hymns which the choristers sang during the performance of their ring dances and three-step dances (*tripudia*). This term *tripudia* involved three steps forward
and one step backward and was used both in ring dances
and in processionals.

A fourteenth-century hymn to the virgin Mary includes
these lines:

94

I greet thee with garlands of roses;
Ah! help us to the heavenly dance
And lead us to the wondrous light,
Which shines from the house of the saved.[42]

In a medieval Spanish hymn to the virgin there are
these lines:

Virgin, thou dost rise to everlasting triumph!
Thou dost rightly share the heavenly ring dance.[43]

In a hymn dedicated to the martyr Ursula the thought
includes not only the ring dance of the angels, but also the
symbolic action of the power of trampling over evil:

Lead thou the host of eleven thousand virgins
In the ring dance of the angels,

. . . .

Trampling vices underfoot.[44]

Priests and members of the congregation participated in
a processional in Moosburg near Munich. The song for this
processional dance was composed by the dean and was in
manuscript form in 1360:

This well-known, highly esteemed act
Brings again our bishop's blessing.
Dispersing as if in the light of dawn
The dark clouds of the depressed mind.

Chorus:
Therefore I free myself
From all sorrow that comes.

. . . .

Numerous hands join and clasp in dance;
This broad and joyous path
Gives ample space for the chain of dancers.

A TIME TO DANCE

Chorus:
> Those who would be lured hence
> To vicious habits are quickly stopped
> And obey . . . willingly and with joy
> The church order.
>
> . . . .
>
> All these festive gestures
> Intend the gift of inward joy.[45]

This song gives insight into the therapy that choral movement brings to those depressed and also into the prevention
of wrongdoing by absorption in harmonious and meaningful activity.

In the fourteenth century there were dances for healing.
One hymn, in which a dance to St. Anthony is suggested,
dates from 1331:

> On this happy pleasant day
> The choristers sing and dance (*tripudio*);
>
> . . . .
>
> They bring in special prayer
> Their praise of St. Anthony.[46]

From the fourteenth to the seventeenth century there
were various dances for curing diseases; some of the participants were suffering diseases, others were hoping to
ward them off. Usually the dances were performed in
honor of the apostle John, St. Vitus, St. Anthony, or the
virgin Mary. It would seem that the dancers found some
relief from pain in the active participation. The full history
of the religious dance as involved in healing during this
period is presented in *Religious Dances in the Christian
Church and in Popular Medicine* by E. Louis Backman.

96

The processional dance at Echternach originated in this period and has survived to the present day. It will be described later in the listing of choral dances that are extant today.

Dance carols were a part of the medieval and Renaissance periods. An Easter carol or ring dance took place in the cloisters on Easter Eve at the church in Sens and is described in a sixteenth-century manuscript. The archbishop assisted and all the clergy as well. They first moved round two by two, followed in the same manner by prominent citizens, all singing songs of the resurrection. Then the carol was performed. It has been described as a *chorea,* but with no hopping. The dance continued from the cloister into the church, round the choir, into the nave, to the singing of the song *Salvator Mundi.*

Similarly the canons and the choristers danced during the Whitsun festival in Chalon-sur-Saône to the singing of *Veni Sancte Spiritus.*

The Dance of Death (*danse macabre*) was the most widely known of all the religious dances from the twelfth to the sixteenth century. It was danced in Italy, Spain, France, Germany, and England. Probably its origin was in the medieval sermons on death. The preaching of the Franciscans and Dominicans emphasized the terrors of death as a means of frightening sinners into repentance. The Dance of Death often started with a sermon on the certainty of death, delivered by a monk, usually in the cemetery or churchyard. Then from the charnel house would come a figure, or in some cases a group of figures, in the traditional attire of Death, which was a close-fitting yellowish suit painted to resemble a skeleton. Victims were

97

invited or coerced into accompanying Death beyond the grave. Death, although grotesque, appeared not as a destroyer but as a messenger summoning men to the world beyond.

During the period of the epidemic of the Black Death, between 1347-73, there was less improvising in the Dance of Death and more of a set pattern evolved with musical accompaniment and a processional design. The whole of medieval society was represented from the pope to the common laborer, and each man, regardless of station, was made an unwilling captive by Death. These people, arranged according to their rank, advanced in processional formation. Death indulged in grotesque and mocking dance positions. An excerpt from a long poem entitled "The Dance of Death," which was written before 1480, suggests the type of lines Death spoke. He is addressing a minstrel who has come within his power:

O thou minstral: that cannest so note and pipe
Unto folkes: for to do pleasaunce
By the right hande anoon I shall thee gripe
With these others: to go upon my daunce
There is no scape; nowther avoydaunce
On no side.[47]

Other lines from French manuscripts bring out the "democratic" mood of the dance, for all people were "equal" before Death:

La Mort:	*Saint-Père (pope), c'est à vous de commencer la Danse. Je veux que le premier on vous voit avancer.*
	. . . .
La Mort:	*Vous qui vivez joyeusement, Ou jeune, ou vieux, vous danserez.*
	. . . .
Le Roy:	*Je n'ai point appris à danser . . . Votre danse est un peu trop sauvage!*
La Mort:	*(au Fou): Ce que dansez n'est en usage, Mais, pauvre sot, bien vous avient, Autant le fou comme le sage, Tout homme à danser il convient!* [48]

A peculiar variation of the Dance of Death arose in 1373. It was connected with wakes for the dead and seemed to have originated from a singing game of Slavonic origin in which the guests paired off to dance and sing. Then when a sudden shrill note came, the music stopped, and in the silence everyone stood still. A moment later when a sad melody was piped, one of the young men fell to the ground as if dead. The girls and women danced around him with mourning gestures as they sang a dirge. "Then one after another bent over the dead man and kissed him back to life

till a general round dance concluded the first half." [49]
Again the death dance was repeated, with the variation that
the boys and men mourned over a young girl. This dance
bore witness to man's sense of mystery over death and his
need to express it symbolically. It is said that this dance was
used as a magic cure for sickness and it may be that people
in the midst of the plague fell back upon this primitive expression in order to find release from their grief and
fear.

The Dance of Death was known in Spain in 1360 as
La Danza General de la Meurte. In Italy, besides the traditional dance, there was a spectacular representation of
death as the all-conqueror in the *Trionfo della Morte*. In
Florence as late as 1559, there was a "Triumph of Death"
procession with an oxen-drawn wagon upon which Death
stood holding his scythe, surrounded by coffins. The processional company sang the *Miserere*. Baumker, in Herder's
Kirchen Lexikon, mentions seven French Dances of Death,
dating back to the fifteenth century, three to the sixteenth,
and three to the seventeenth centuries. There were five
Dances of Death known in England. John Lydgate, in the
early part of the fifteenth century, wrote *The Dance of
Death*. Samples of the dramatic *Dance of Death* are found
in the Altsfeld Passion Plays, in *Charité* (French morality
play), and in the Neumarket Passion Play. There have
been numerous illustrations of the Dance of Death on the
walls of cemeteries or charnel houses, in mortuary chapels,
and even in churches throughout Europe. One of the oldest
pictures was painted in 1425 in the *Cimetière des Innocents* near Paris. Another famous one is "The Triumph of
Death" in the cemetery of Pisa, painted between 1450 and

1500. Holbein became interested in the Dance of Death, and in 1538 he made a series of drawings to illustrate the dance. Even in the twentieth century it has a hold on the imaginative mind, for in "The Green Table," danced by the Jooss Ballet, there is a modern *danse macabre* as Death dances on the battlefield sowing destruction.

In the medieval period an ecstatic dancing sect, the *Chorizantes,* sprang up in Germany with a membership in the thousands, including both sexes. They would dance through the streets and in and out of churches until they were exhausted. They were not interested in the attention of spectators, but absorbed in their fantastic visions. For example, they might imagine that they were wading in a stream of blood, and in interpretive action, they would leap wildly in the air as if to get out of the blood. These dances first appeared during the festival of John the Baptist at midsummer in Aachen in 1374. They then spread to Cologne and Metz and other parts of Germany.

A similar display of ecstatic dancing occurred at Strasbourg in 1419. Here St. Vitus was invoked to cure a malady. St. Vitus was martyred under Diocletian in the third century. The tradition is that he had cured the emperor's son of demonic possession. He became the patron saint of nervous diseases and his dance was considered of curative value. Gradually the name of St. Vitus became connected with the disease chorea.

The most ancient of the Christianized pagan dances were the fire dances which later became the dance of St. John's Day and the dance of "Brandons." The St. John's dance was celebrated on the eve of June 24 in Brittany, Provence, and England, and is still preserved in remote places. In this bonfire dance the celebrants leaped over or through the fire. It is suggested that perhaps this had an ancient health value because the smoke and flames tended to destroy vermin and miasma. The "Brandons," an ancient torch dance accompanied by chants and prayers, was performed on the first of May and at Pentecost. But Pentecost was also celebrated in a more devout way by the canons of Chalon-sur-Saône, who had the custom of dancing *in prato* on the evening of Pentecost to the accompaniment of chants, beginning with *Veni Sancte Spiritus.* Nevertheless, this custom was abolished in 1624.

Through the centuries, councils were alert to curtail excesses in sacred dancing: Auxerre (573), Toledo (589), Chalon-sur-Saône (639), Rome (826), Avignon (1209), and Paris (1212). The pagan element that was present and the undisciplined mass participation made it difficult for the consecrated and controlled religious dance to continue. The sacred dance had been overshadowed by the frenzied and grotesque Dances of Death, the wild exhausting dances of the *Chorizantes,* and the leaping torch dances.

THE RENAISSANCE (1400-1700)

The Renaissance, which developed in the early fifteenth century, is said to have begun with Dante (1265-1321). In the *Divine Comedy,* Dante refers to dancing as the occupation of those in paradise: " 'Hosanna! Lord God of Sabaoth!' . . . Thus, revolving to its own melody, that substance was seen by me to sing, and it and the others moved in their dance." [50] Again he describes the blessed ones as dancing in such various measures that some seemed to stand still and some to fly: "And as wheels within the fittings of clocks revolve, so that to him who gives heed the first seems quiet, and the last to fly, *so these carols, differently dancing,* swift and slow, made me rate their riches." [51]

This conception of heavenly dancing is similar to that of Bonaventura (*ca.* 1260) described in his chapter "Of the Joys of Paradise" in *Dieta Salutis*: "In that celestial dance there is one who leadeth the whole dance, so doth the Christ (this sacred circling); 'tis he who will be *leader of the dance, leading that company most blessed and preceding it.*" It was such vision of the highest in this art that became a guide for the creation of sacred dances during the Renaissance.

Elaborate and dramatic presentations became popular at this time and the dance was an integral part of most of them. Allegorical masques made use of symbolic dancing to heighten the dramatic moods. In England, to celebrate the return of Henry V after his victory at Agincourt in 1415, maidens danced with tambourines. As they sang and danced the people were reminded of David's triumph. Another instance of the dance being used in a court celebration was in 1432 in London, in a pageant to honor Henry VI during the festive time following his coronation. In this pageant there were seven maidens representing the seven celestial virtues, and another seven representing the terrestrial virtues. At an appointed time "the entire choir of fourteen, clapping their hands and breaking into *tripudia* (dances) sang welcome hymns." [52]

Corpus Christi processions were originally nothing more than ambulatory dances in which the participants, following a certain pattern, bowed in measure, swung censers in cadence, and threw flowers into the air. In 1463, King René

sponsored in Provence an elaborate Corpus Christi masque which was called *Lou Gué* and also *Jeux de la Fête-Dieu*. It was presented as a series of scenes on pageant wagons. The dramatizations used no dialogue, only pantomime and dancing. One of the scenes showed the Jews dancing round the golden calf; another was of King Herod being persecuted by devils who were after his soul; at the end came Death with a scythe.

That dance is inspired from an inward, spiritual source was clear to Guglielmo Ebreo, a Jewish dancing master (*ca.* 1480). He writes:

104

Dancing is an action, showing outwardly the spiritual movements which must agree with those measures and perfect concords of harmony, which, through our hearing and with earthly joy, descend into one's intellect, there to produce sweet movements, which, being thus imprisoned, as it were, in defiance of nature, endeavor to escape and reveal themselves through movement. . . . The art of dancing is for generous hearts that love it, for gentle spirits that have a heaven-sent inclination for it. It is a matter entirely different from and mortally inimical . . . to the depraved minds [which] turn it from a liberal art and virtuous science, into a vile, adulterous affair.[53]

Here is a clear statement of the problem involved in the art of the dance—how it may develop as "a liberal art and a virtuous science" and yet not become low or vulgar.

St. Teresa (*ca.* 1555) danced at Carmel in holy joy. In the seventeenth century two other noted Carmelites imitated this Spanish saint—Bienheureuse Marie de l'Incarnation and second sister Anne de Jésus who danced before *le Saint Sacrement* at Carmel in Dijon.

In the beautiful paintings of the Renaissance there are glimpses of movement as the angels represent adoration. The flow of the costumes, the positions held for the moment, and the circular formations, all imply that the artists conceived of movement rather than static positions. The circling dance may have been connected with the "carols" of this period, for the term carol was the name given by the *trouvères* to a dance in which the performers moved slowly in a circle, singing as they went. Fra Angelico (1387-1455) painted "the Dance of the Redeemed" as part of "The Last Judgment," [54] portraying a circular dance of saints and angels entering paradise. Ethel Urlin quotes a translation of a poem, *Il Ballo dei Angeli,* as descriptive of this scene:

A TIME TO DANCE

Dance they in a ring in heaven
All the blessed in that garden
Where the love divine abideth
Which is all aglow with love.
In that ring dance all the blessed
In that ring dance all the angels
Go they before the Bridegroom
Dance, all of them for love.
In that court is joyfulness
Of a love that's fathomless.
All of them go to the dancing
For the Savior whom they love.[55]

Botticelli (*ca.* 1487) portrayed angels dancing in a circle
above the Nativity scene. And the composer of *In Dulci
Jubilo* is said to have dreamed of angels dancing as they
sang, and upon waking he wrote down the melody of the
carol.

In Renée Foatelli's *The Religious Dances in Christianity*, there is a photograph of the sculptural work *Danse d'église (Ronde sur ivoire)* of the fourteenth century. It shows a group of young women holding hands in a circling formation. Donatello's "Dance of the Angels" [56] portrays angels in symbolic movement. The artists of the Renaissance reveal the serenity and adoration expressed in the sacred dances of their time.

Although religious dances continued to flourish during the Renaissance, certain events occurred that were to have a crippling effect upon this art. Books began to be printed after 1455, and, with the printing of tracts, pamphlets, and books, there was a growing emphasis upon the intellect. The mind would soon be considered as all-important and the body as valueless in religious growth. The Reformation, which began about 1517, would tend in its extreme forms to do away with most of the visual arts, leaving only the arts of printing, preaching, and music. It would soon abolish all dances and processions, except the funeral procession.

Martin Luther (*ca.* 1525), who loved children, wrote many carols for them. In his carol "From Heaven High" there are two little-known stanzas:

> A little child for you this morn
> Has from a chosen maid been born,
> A little child so tender, sweet,
> That you should skip upon your feet.
>
> I can play the whole day long.
> I'll dance and sing for you a song,
> A soft and soothing lullaby
> So sweet that you will never cry.[57]

Evidently Martin Luther understood the natural way that a child expresses joy spontaneously with his whole being—singing, skipping, and dancing. Luther was adamant against whatever was sham or pretense, but he loved what was genuine and real and brought about the total involvement of a dedicated person, whether a child or an adult.

William Tyndale in his Prologue to the New Testament writes: "Euagelio (that we cal gospel) is a greke word, and signyfyth good, mery, glad and ioyfull tydings, that maketh a mannes hert glad, and maketh hym synge, daunce, and leepe for ioye." This sixteenth-century English church leader was not fearful of using the dramatic verbs "daunce" and "leepe" when he considered the joy of the good news in the New Testament.

The Council of Trent (1545-63), which represented the Roman Catholic Counter-Reformation, showed a determination to return to the liturgical tradition of the Middle Ages and so it removed many literary and dramatic interpolations. The statutes of the synod meeting at Lyons in 1566 threatened priests and other persons with excommunication if they led dances in churches or cemeteries. The church was determined to stop religious dancing, but the dancing continued in a variety of forms.

The Renaissance courts with their love of display often sponsored dances of a semireligious nature. The pavane, a stately dance, was usually performed at the time of the death of someone in the court circle, especially in the case of a young lady. (In recent years, Ravel composed "A Pavane for a Dead Princess.") William Dunbar, in 1507, describes a "Dance of the Seven Deadly Sins" at the Edinburgh court on the day before fastern's e'en as a combination of the dance of death with a morality masque.[58]

When Catherine de Medici came to France she brought with her a taste for Italian dancing and she sponsored masked dances done to the accompaniment of psalms. In 1572 Catherine produced an exciting dance-drama called "The Defense of Paradise." The dramatic clash portrayed is between the Roman Catholic king of France (Charles IX) and his brothers, who are attempting to defend heaven, and the Protestant king of Navarre and his friends, who are guarding hell. The knights, commanded by Navarre, attack those defending heaven. The fight, which had been planned in advance, leaves the victory to Charles IX, and his assailants are thrown back to hell, which swallows them. "After a long ballet, victors and vanquished joined each other in paradise." [59]

Such theatrical dance must have been rehearsed many times. It is amazing to think that in this period when men were bitterly hostile the art of music and dancing could project, for a short while at least, an attitude of mutual respect and honor. How ironical this situation was—for the production of "The Defense of Paradise" was presented on the eighteenth of August, and six days later came St. Bartholomew's Day and the massacre! So the artistic hope of reconciliation was lost. The conflict had become too bitter to be healed by the arts.

In 1588 a defense of religious dancing was written by Thoinot Arbeau. He says:

For one who has spoken ill of dances, there are an infinity of others who have praised and esteemed them. The holy and royal prophet David danced before the ark of the Lord. And as for the holy prophet Moses, he was not angered to witness dancing, but grieved because it was performed round a golden calf, which was idolatry. In the early church there was a custom which has endured until our time to sing the hymns of our faith while dancing, and this may still be observed in some places.[60]

One such place was the cathedral in York, England, where up to the seventeenth century there was dancing in the nave on Shrove Tuesday.

Dancing was an integral part of the first oratorio. This oratorio, *La Rappresentazione di Anima e di Corpo* by Emilio de' Cavalieri, performed in the oratory of the Chiesa S. Maria in Vallicella in Rome in 1600. The principal characters were Time, the World, Life, Pleasure, the Intellect, the Soul, the Body. The following stage directions show how the original oratorio is made varied and dramatic through symbolic dances:

> The verse beginning *Chiostri altissimi estellati* must be sung accompanied by stately and reverent steps. To these will succeed other grave steps and figures of a solemn character. During the *ritornelli* the four principal dancers will perform a ballet embellished with capers without singing. And thus, after each verse, the steps of the dance will always be varied, the four chief dancers sometimes using the *gagliarde,* sometimes the *cenario,* and sometimes the *corrente* which will do well in the *ritornelli.*[61]

A traditional Easter dance, the bergerette, was performed annually in the churches of the diocese of Besançon on the afternoon of Easter Day. In a book of rites of the Church of Ste Marie Magdaleine in 1582, there is a chapter on Easter Day which contains the following: "At the end of the sermon . . . there are dances (*chorea*) in the cloister or in the middle of the nave of the church if it is rainy weather; they are danced to certain airs contained in the processional [chant books]." [62] In regard to the figure of the dance, there is this description:

> The canons held hands in a ring; behind them was a second ring composed of choirboys, each paired with a canon, while in the center was the chief dignitary, the senior in rank with the smallest chorister in attendance. After this, the circle broke up, and the oldest and youngest led the way in a serpentine or labyrinthine dance. [63]

In spite of synodal diocesan decrees of 1585 and 1601 that threatened severe penalties against the enthusiasts who ventured to keep up the ancient custom, the dance continued in the churches of Besançon until 1738. By 1647 the dance had become less intricate, as is obvious from a description which states that all the participants went to the cloisters where they held one another's hands and then proceeded to make "three circuits around the cloisters."

The dance songs that were used had originated in the fourteenth century. They consisted of couplets, with repetitions arranged to suit the dance. Mead offers one in translation from the Latin:

> Let the sober voice of the faithful sound,
> Turn round and round, O Sion, with joy;
> Let there be but one rejoicing of all
> Who have been redeemed by one only grace;
> Turn round and about, O Sion, with joy. [64]

The notation of the manuscript is in the usual form of the plainsong:

si	si	la	sol	la	ut	ut	ut	ut	si	la	si
Con	*vert*	*er*	*e*	*Si*	*on*	*in*	*gau*	*di*	—	—	*a.*

The arrangement of the air, however, is in keeping with the branle, a courtly dance in which one couple leads the rest.

The art of the dance was accepted as an integral part of all special ceremonies. Sir John Davies, in his poem "Orchestra" (1594), writes of this:

Stanza 77
Since when all ceremonius mysteries,
All sacred orgies and religious rights,
All pomps, and triumphs, and solemnities,
All funerals, nuptials, and like publike sights,
All parliaments of peace, and warlike fights,
  All learned arts, and every great affaire
  A lively shape of Daucing seemes to beare.

Later in the poem he suggests there were many dance-dramas and that the directions were known for their presentation. Also he reveals that new designs were constantly being created for these religious dances.

Stanza 86
Thus they who first did found a common-weale,
And they who first Religion did ordaine
By dauncing first the peoples hearts did steale,
Of whome we now a thousand tales doe faine,
Yet doe we now their perfect rules retaine,
  And use them still in such devices new
  As in the world long since their withering grew.

Among the numerous religious dances created for special occasions in this period are the *ballet ambulatoire* to celebrate the canonization of Cardinal Carlo Borromeo in 1610, the dance to celebrate the canonization of Ignatius of Loyola in 1622, and the "moral ballet" composed in 1634 to commemorate the birthday of the cardinal of Savoy. The

112

word ballet implied a professional dance group for theatrical performance.

The term choir in this period meant an enclosed, elevated area in the church where symbolic movements were often portrayed. In 1682 Ménestrier, a Jesuit in Paris, describes the use of the choir:

> The divine office was made up of psalms, hymns, and canticles for the praises of God were recited, sung, and danced. . . . The place where these religious acts were performed in divine worship was called the choir, just as with the *choroi* of the Greeks. In Latin, the prelates were called *praesules,* . . . for in the choir, at the divine office, they played the same part as the leader of the dances.[65]

Ménestrier goes on to explain that in early times the choir was separated from the altar, and raised up so as to form a stage which was enclosed by a breast-high screen. This type of choir can still be seen in the churches of SS. Clement and Pancras at Rome.

"The dance," says Raffaello delle Colombe, a Dominican monk in 1622, "is a symbol of the universal order and can be compared with the dance of the stars. For prayer is a spiritual dance. . . . God leads the ring dance of the heavenly bodies. God leads inside the ring." [66]

A unique dance was performed by priests at Eastertime in the cathedrals of Auxerre, Reims, Rouen, Sens, Narbonne, and generally throughout France. The unusual feature of the dance was that it centered upon the tossing of a ball (pelota or *pilota*).[67] When the *pilota* had been received from the canon or dean, the priests began to intone antiphonally the sequence appropriate to the Easter festival: "Praises to the Pascal Victim." Then, supporting the ball with his left hand, he began to dance in time with the rhythmical sounds of the chanted sequence, while the rest, holding hands, executed a choral dance round the labyrinth. Meanwhile the *pilota* was handed or thrown alternately by the dean to the dancers. The passing of the ball backward and forward, in the circular dance, in which every dancer also revolved on his own axis, may well have been thought to illustrate the apparent path or dance of the sun in the heavens throughout the year and so of its "passion."

The dance at Auxerre included a variety of symbolic patterns: the resurrection of Christ—sun, the cosmic mystery of the heavenly bodies, and the labyrinthine dance.

In Cornwall, England, there was a carol which probably went back to the time of the medieval minstrels and troubadours. This "Cornwall Carol" seems to have a peculiar mixture of religious carol and folk song; it tells the story of the life of Christ in ballad form, as if related by Jesus:

> Tomorrow shall be my dancing day,
> I would my true love did so chance
> To see the legend of my play,
> To call my true love to my dance.
>   Sing, O my love, O my love, my love, my love;
>   This have I done for my true love.
>
> Then was I born of a virgin pure,
> Of her I took fleshly substance;
> Thus was I knit to man's nature,
> To call my true love to my dance.
>   Sing, O my love, O my love, my love, my love;
>   This have I done for my true love.

The ballad develops such incidents as the birth in the

manger, the baptism, the temptations in the desert, the be-
trayal by Judas, and the trial before Pilate:

> Before Pilate the Jews me brought
> When Barabbas had deliverance;
> They scourgèd me and set me at nought,
> Judged me to die to lead the dance.
>> Sing, O my love, O my love, my love, my love;
>> This have I done for my true love.

After telling of the death on the cross and the descent into
hell, the ballad closes with:

> Then up to heaven I did ascend,
> Where now I dwell in sure substance
> On the right hand of God, that man
> May come unto the general dance.
>> Sing, O my love, O my love, my love, my love;
>> This have I done for my true love.[68]

It is possible that as the church gradually closed its door
to religious dances, remnants of them became parts of folk
songs. The stanzas of the "Cornwall Carol" show an intel-
ligent development of the life of Christ which must have
had its origin within the church. Robert Shaw has presented three stanzas of this carol in his recordings of Christmas music.

Another Christmas carol that is sung today, "Joseph
Dearest, Joseph Mine," was written down in this period. It
was then known as *Resonnet in laudibus,* and dancing was
part of the carol. In a church near Leipzig there was a
dance with symbolic movements of rocking the Christchild
in the cradle during the singing of *Resonnet in laudibus.*
Boys and girls danced about and some of the adults did too.

Johannes Boemus, in 1520, tells of Christmas Eve dances in the churches of old Franconia: "With what rejoicing did not only the priests, but also the people, celebrate in the churches the birth of Christ. . . . They placed on the altar a doll representing the Christchild, after which the boys and girls hopped a ring dance around the altar." [69]

Later, in the sixteenth century, when the *Resonnet* was sung at a vesper service, small boys hopped up and down and clapped their hands to show their joy at the birth of Christ.

Another dance-carol, "Dance of the Child Jesus," was held at Roquebrussanne near Brignoles, and the dance was continued up to the twentieth century. Little babies took part in it, especially those who were retarded in learning to walk. After high mass, on the day of the patronal feast of the church, the mothers with their babies formed a group around the altar of the Christchild and one of them began to sing:

116

Dance on the right foot,
Dance on the left foot,
  My good Jesus,
Dance on both feet.

The words of the song were accompanied by appropriate steps and gestures.

There were also carols for ring dances at the time of a death. A churchyard dance was sung by the girls as they returned to the church from the grave of a friend. The music and words were copied in 1840 in Bailleul, Flanders:

In heaven there is a dance. Alleluia.
Where all the maidens dance.
May the Lord bless us. Alleluia. Alleluia.
It is for Amelia. Alleluia.
We dance like those young maidens.
May the Lord bless us! Alleluia.[70]

Another variation from Bailleul, as recorded by Ethel Urlin, is:

'Tis for Rosalie they sing,
Alleluia.
She is done with sorrowing—
So we dance and we sing so,
Benedicamus Domino,
Alleluia, Alleluia.[71]

In an old Christian tomb inscription there is this reference to joy in death:

No sorrowful tears, no beating of the breast
For a safe repose has taken me. I dance
Ring dances with the blessed saints
In the beautiful fields of the righteous.[72]

A TIME TO DANCE

In these fragments of funeral ring-dance songs or carols there is a glimpse into the custom of using choral movement to express the deep joy-in-sorrow which is a Christian attitude. Here was the expression of joy in the release of the soul into the immortal life.

It has been suggested that the song

> Ring around a Rosie
> Pockets full of posies;
> Ashes, ashes,
> All fall down.

is not just a "children's song" but a remnant of an early carol around a grave. "Ring *around*," "Rosie" for Rosalie, "posies" or flowers to place or toss onto the grave! Where are the words "ashes to ashes" used except in the graveside service of the liturgical churches. The circling stops on the words "ashes, ashes"; "all fall down" suggests the act of kneeling at the close of the funeral carol. A remembrance of *Domino* could be in the word down. This children's ring dance that exists today may have come down from an early English churchyard practice of circling about a grave.

Among the Slavonic peoples there was the *kolo*, which was danced in the churchyard in connection with funerals. The participants held hands and in this case they formed a line and danced backward.

An Easter hymn by Palestrina (*ca.* 1590) suggests the triumphant power of immortal life. There is joy in the "alleluias," release because "the strife is o'er" and "the song of triumph has begun." Exaltation is expressed in the line "Let shouts of holy joy outburst: Alleluia." Perhaps funeral services could have a more Christian character if, instead of

mourning over the departed, there could be joyous acceptance of death as an onward step toward immortal life. As
Winfred Rhoades says, "*Alleluia* is the proper note for mark-
ing the progress of one who advances from this temporary
abiding place." [73] The organist Charles Widor, in his
Marche Funèbre et Chante Seraphique, has expressed the
sorrow-joy elements in death. If the funeral must be expressed somberly, let the angel song of spiritual bliss not
be forgotten. The traditional antiphon following the "Mass
for the Dead"

> *In paradisum deducant te Angeli:*
> *In tuo adventu suscipiant te Martyres,* . . .
> *Chorus Angelorum te suscipiat.* . . .

has preserved the radiant Christian faith in the spiritual
immortality of the soul as it is received into the joy of paradise by a choir of angels.

POST-RENAISSANCE PERIOD (1700-1900)

Although sacred dance had flourished during the Renaissance in the oratorio, in the interpretation of hymns and
psalms in services of worship, and in theatrical allegorical
ballets, in the post-Renaissance period the door was firmly
closed on its creative expression. Neither the Roman Catholic Church nor the Protestant Christian churches would
allow sacred dances in their services. Religious dancing either disappeared, survived in isolated places, changed into
folk expressions, or remained submerged in the prescribed
movements of the mass itself.

As the Roman Catholic Church became more centrally
authoritative in Rome and published conforming edicts,

there was little chance for creative and fresh exploration in the sacred dance. Backman lists in chronological order a survey of the prohibitive decrees of various councils, synods, and officials of the church from the fourth century to the eighteenth century. At the conclusion of the survey he writes:

> Dancing by the clergy was eventually stopped, except certain choristers' dances in Spain; but the church was never able to suppress the popular church dances. It was only the Reformation, with its highly critical attitude toward traditional church customs and its fight against images, . . . the worship of saints, and pilgrimages, which ultimately succeeded in suppressing the church dance.[74]

The Protestant Christian churches at the time of the Reformation had banished the arts of painting, sculpture, and drama from any functions connected with their churches, and had stifled any manifestations of religious dancing. The Puritans went even farther, for they frowned on all drama and all dance as the sport of the devil. In general, Protestant Christians felt that the portals of the spirit were to be entered with great seriousness through the mind and not through the senses. However, even in this strictness, some of the leaders were intellectually aware of the religious dances mentioned in the Old Testament. John Cotton, a New England Puritan, writes, "Dancing I would not simply condemn, for I see two sorts of mixt dancing in use with God's people in the Old Testament; the one religious (Exodus 15:20-21), the other civil, tending to the praise of conquerors (1 Samuel 18:6-7)." [75] In his discourse "An Arrow Against Profane and Promiscuous Dancing," [76] Increase Mather, another Puritan, condemned only dancing that aroused the passions. But, in general, all conventional Protestant Christians came to assume that religious dancing might be done by "primitive savages" or "benighted pagans," but never—absolutely never—by Christians.

Thus, by the eighteenth century, religious dances were scarce and scattered. In Venice, during a Procession of the Rosary, the dancers represented a triple rosary which moved around in harmonious designs. In Messina, another sacred procession was performed to celebrate the Assumption of the Virgin. This included wagons with allegorical scenes in which there were choreographic interpretations. Jacques Cambry, a French archaeologist, reports in *Un Voyage dans le Finistère* (1794) that he had seen dancing in the chapel and in the cemetery near Brest in Brittany in 1766. In Liége, on the Tuesday of Pentecost, a choral dance was performed in the cathedral of St. Lambert until 1794.

In England there had been dances to carols in country churches. In the sixteenth century, during the reign of Queen Elizabeth I, men and women had danced to the music of pipes and drums both inside and outside churches and in churchyards. In the seventeenth century, students and servants in York had danced in the nave of the cathedral on Shrove Tuesday. The annual dance in Salisbury Cathedral survived into the eighteenth century. It was part of an ancient custom celebrated by the inhabitants of Wishford and Batford.

In Belgium, in the eighteenth century, the students of Huy's College near Liége used to dance in the college chapel at the beginning of Lent.

In the nineteenth century there were a few accounts of choral dances for special days. One of them describes a

Corpus Christi processional dance in Onna, Spain. Twelve young men grouped in twos moved around the sacrament.

> When the procession started, they knelt before the sacrament and then began their dance, advancing among the devout spectators. They danced in a . . . more rapid tempo ahead of the procession. After a while they turned and, as it were, flew back to the sacrament and knelt down before it. Then, the dance began again; it was a . . . real *tripudium*. Backward and forward they swayed and knelt before the sacrament. It reminds us again of David's dance before the ark.[77]

The celebration of the Ascension of the Virgin Mary on August 15 in Alaro in the Balearic Islands included a church dance in which six young choristers, called *les cosiers,* dramatized the clash of good and evil. Three were in white, adorned with colored ribbons and carrying flower-decorated birettas; one was dressed as the virgin Mary; two were costumed as devils with horns. Following the procession, the six *cosiers* danced around the image of Mary. This mystery dance dramatized the power of the virgin Mary and the angels in overcoming the lurking devils—the power of good triumphant over evil.

But these expressions of symbolic movement were the exceptions. Aside from the influences of the churches, the nineteenth-century culture was focused on intellectual and scientific investigation. In general, art was considered "of little practical value" and the dance—mostly ballet and court dances—was looked upon as light entertainment. People felt mental activity was so superior to any physical expression that the dance was relegated to the nonessential list and evaluated as even vulgar and primitive.

Cults and sects. With no opportunity for creative life in

conventional churches, the sacred dance faded out and became unknown to church attendants. However, some sects and cults arose in this arid period and their members experimented with symbolic movements in their rituals.

One of these new cults was a sacred order called "The Free and Accepted Masons," which was organized in 1717. It grew out of a guild meeting of masons who were building English cathedrals. The moral code of the Masons was based on the symbols of the level, the compass, and the plumb, and God was described as the Great Architect of the Universe. In this secret society—as in other later societies, such as the International Order of Odd Fellows and the Grange—elaborate rituals were developed in connection with initiation ceremonies and the attaining of degrees. The members sat around the edge of the hall, leaving the center for special marches and the execution of floor patterns of specific designs. The members found value in participating in the marches and formations, for it provided them with a bond of common action. Each one felt that he had a special place to fill. For many members, the secret order had a stronger hold than the church, which usually asked its attendants merely to sit still and listen.

The Shakers were a unique group that created intricate religious dances. They were founded in 1747 in England. In 1774 a handful of members came as colonists to Niskeyuna, near Albany, New York. The sect grew rapidly after the Revolution and spread through the East and the Midwest. It numbered about six thousand followers in 1850, but since then it has been decreasing until now there are only a few active communities.

The Shakers welcomed all who were tired of "futile

creeds, formal worship, and the evils of a corrupt society."
Their beliefs were derived from certain Huguenot groups
whose ideas descended from the Albigenses of the thirteenth
century, whose adherents in turn had used dance as a way
of adoration. This fact sheds some light on their dance
formations which resemble those of the early Christian
church. In England, the early Shakers walked the floor
while singing and swiftly passed and repassed each other
"like clouds agitated by a mighty wind." The term Shaker
came from the rapid up and down movement of the hands
with the action mostly in the wrists. When the participants
shook their hands with the palms turned down toward the
floor, the symbolic motion meant that they were shaking
out "all that is carnal." When the palms were turned upward as if to receive spiritual blessing, the quick up and
down, shaking movement expressed the open petition
"Come, life eternal." Aside from this common motion of
the hands, there were many pantomimic gestures to interpret their songs. General movements included bowing,
bending, and a great deal of turning, for this motion symbolized turning away from evil and around toward good:

> I'll turn, turn, turn, turn away from all evil,
> And come, come, come, come into the gospel.[78]

In the song " 'Tis the Gift to Be Simple," which Aaron
Copland wove into *Appalachian Spring*, these movements
are mentioned:

> When true simplicity is gain'd,
> To bow and to bend we shan't be asham'd,
> To turn, turn will be our delight
> Till by turning, turning we come round right.[79]

124

This emphasis on turning is reminiscent of the song in the bergerette of 1742: "Turn round and round, O Sion with joy."

The first ordered dance of the Shakers was introduced by Joseph Meacham about 1785. It was the "Square Order Shuffle," patterned according to legend on Father Joseph's vision of angels dancing around the throne of God. In the "Square Order Shuffle," which was called "a solemn exercise," there was a "forward and backward movement of ranks, the brethren and sisters in separate groups shuffling toward and away from each other, three paces each way, with a doublestep or 'tip-tap' at the turn." [80] In 1820 a variation was introduced—men and women shuffled forward and backward in a series of parallel lines, weaving, in imaginative design, a fabric of union and love.

Circling dances were popular at this time. Sometimes there were alternate circles of men and women, with the symbolism of Ezekiel's wheel in the middle of a wheel (Ezekiel 1:16). Walt Whitman, witnessing a "wheel" dance about 1853, said that the singing in the center represented "the harmony and perfection to which all tend and there is God." By 1847 some of the patterns for the Shaker group dances were as follows: winding march, lively line, lively ring, square check, double square, moving square, cross and diamond, finished cross, square and compass. Sometimes they formed a "continuous ring" in the shape of a C moving in serpentine fashion. These group dances became traditional for the Shakers.

Always there was a growing edge of creativity afforded in the pantomimic gestures and rhythmic movements of "stand dances" done in place. Every created faculty, they contended—the hands, the feet, the tongue, the whole body—should "express outwardly and assist the inward reverence of the soul."

> With ev'ry gift I will unite
> And join in sweet devotion;
> To worship God is my delight,
> With hands and feet in motion.[81]

Often there were "merry measures" done to a bounding, elastic step "to quicken the spiritual elements and to stir up zeal." Perhaps it was this type that George Meredith had seen among the English Shakers and described in "Jump to Glory, Jane":

> They jumped the question, jumped reply;
> And whether to insist, deny,
> Reprove, persuade, they jump in ranks.[82]

126

The artist Benson Lossing (1850) could see beauty in the rhythmic movements of the Shakers. He writes:

> Their movements in the dance or march whether natural or studied are all graceful and appropriate; and as I gazed upon that congregation of four or five hundred worshipers marching and countermarching in perfect time, I felt that . . . the involuntary exclamation of even the hypercritical would be, "How beautiful!"

Theirs was a folk art with all participating.

The Shakers were a dedicated group of Christians—industrious, creative, joyous, striving to build an ideal community and contributing rare religious dances. They welcomed Indians and Negroes, for their society was a genuine Christian democracy. Some of their songs are in "pidgin English."

> Now see how spry me dance,
> How nimble me can labor.
>
> . . . .
>
> Me will bow and me will turn
> And dat will mux old nature,
> Den me hab de holy lub
> And dat be much de better.[83]

The Shakers followed an early ruling of the religious group that there should be no marrying among believers. Also, they expected the Second Coming of Christ, much as the first-century Christians did. Their theocracy kept them apart from the world and they failed to get their sect established in home-centered communities. Thus their contribution to the Christian church was limited. However, the Shaker songs and dances are invaluable for use in informal work with present-day movement choirs.

Referring to his recent folk ballad "Lord of the Dance," Sydney Carter of London, England, writes in a letter (1967), "The Shakers more than anybody led me to write this song. . . . After hearing 'The Gift to Be Simple' sung and [seeing it] danced, in a rather stately fashion, . . . at a folk dance festival, I wrote 'Lord of the Dance.' " The ballad is sung to Mr. Carter's adaptation of " 'Tis the Gift to Be Simple."

I danced in the morning when the world was begun,
And I danced in the moon and the stars and the sun
And I came down from heaven and I danced on the earth;
At Bethlehem I had my birth.

Chorus:
Dance then wherever you may be;
I am the Lord of the dance, said he,
And I'll lead you all wherever you may be,
And I'll lead you all in the dance, said he.

I danced for the scribe and Pharisee,
But they would not dance and they wouldn't follow me.
I danced for the fishermen, for James and John;
They came with me and the dance went on.

I danced on the sabbath and I cured the lame;
The holy people said it was a shame.
They whipped and they stripped and they hung me high
And they left me there on a cross to die.

I danced on a Friday when the sky turned black;
It's hard to dance with the devil on your back.
They buried my body and they thought I'd gone,
But I am the dance and I still go on.

They cut me down and I leap up high;
I am the life that'll never, never die.
I'll live in you if you'll live in me;
I am the Lord of the dance, said he.[84]

A TIME TO DANCE

A revival of interest. At the close of the nineteenth century symbolic movement was not acceptable in the established churches. However, an Anglo-Catholic, who may have had some influence among the leaders of the Church of England, had started a growing edge of exploration in the use of interpretive movement in the liturgy.

By 1884, in England, Stewart Headlam expressed his interest in drama by directing a group of girls who participated in special services. In the October, 1884, issue of the *Church Reformer*, he writes:

> The art of dancing, . . . perhaps more than all other arts, is an outward and visible sign of an inward and spiritual grace, ordained by the Word of God himself, as a means whereby we receive the same and a pledge to assure us thereof; and [it] has suffered even more than the other arts from the utter anti-sacramentalism of British philistia. Your Manichaean Protestant, and your superfine rationalist, reject the dance as worldly, frivolous, sensual, and so forth; and your dull, stupid sensualist sees legs, and grunts with some satisfaction; but your sacramentalist knows something worth more than both of these. He knows what perhaps the dancer herself may be partially unconscious of, that we live now by faith and not by sight, and that the poetry of dance is the expression of unseen spiritual grace.

What rejoicing in heaven may be his as the sacred dance has continued to develop throughout the world during the years since Stewart Headlam began its revival!

INTO THE TWENTIETH CENTURY

A few remnants of religious dances have lasted into the twentieth century. Besides the dance of *los seises,* which has been described previously, there is a well-known annual festival in Echternach, Luxembourg, where a processional dance in honor of St. Willibrord continues in its traditional form since the fourteenth century and possibly earlier.[85] It is held at Whitsuntide. A great procession assembles outside the town of Echternach, crosses the bridge, and progresses through the main street and up the long flight of steps leading to the churchyard. The procession is preceded by the priests and choristers carrying the processional cross and banners; then come the children and youths, and after them the hosts of pilgrims, sometimes as many as two or three thousand. Some of the pilgrims are sick with epilepsy and other diseases; some are healthy and they dance for the sick at home or for those unable to dance. The relics of St. Willibrord have been considered effective in healing; they are buried beneath the altar in the church.

The processional is danced by the participants taking three steps forward and one back, or three or four steps to the right and three or four steps to the left executed in a diagonal direction. Every time the backward or forward movement is changed the processional stops for a moment, the knees are raised high, and then the feet stamp down. For this reason the processional has been called a hopping and a standing dance. The body swings from side to side and the arms move in balancing motions.

Upon entering the church the participants continue to dance up the right aisle to the choir area and the altar, where they kneel and kiss some part of the altar. Then they dance around the altar and back down the left aisle and out into the churchyard.

Another dance that has survived into the present in Barcelona, Valencia, and Majorca is the "Dance of the Eagles." Usually this dance appears in the Corpus Christi processions and also inside the church. In the choir area two "eagles," representing John the Baptist, dance and advance to the altar, where they continue to dance. In earlier times the dancers were dressed as birds and wore head masks; but nowadays the dancers carry the models of eagles' heads.

An altar dance, in Barcelona, is performed by six couples who are clad in bright colors and dance a solemn "candle dance." The women, who hold glass bowls containing water and some flowers, move in the inner circle, surrounded by the outer circle of men. Traditionally the men carried candles. This dance was intended for the adorning of the altar in honor of SS. Victor and Aetius. Other remnants of sacred dances in Spain are described by Backman.

The wedding dance has been traditional throughout Europe and is still performed in the Greek Orthodox churches. It is a ring dance about the altar at the conclusion of the ceremony. Usually the six participants are the priest, the best man, the bridegroom, the bride, the bridesmaid, and the deacon. They join hands in this order to perform their sacred wedding dance.

In the Coptic Christian churches in Ethiopia the early dances still exist. The liturgy of the Coptic Christian Church was founded in the Alexandrine rites, which had the support of Basil and Gregory of Nazianzus, both of whom had shown interest in the sacred dances of the early church. Festival dances performed in September and in January are described by an observer:

First there is low-pitched singing without musical accompaniment, . . . then come the cymbals, and finally the big drums. Meantime the long line of priests advances and retires and others turn first to one side and then to another, swaying their bodies to the rhythm of the music. More and more people join the dance; the tempo quickens and voices are raised to a climax. Then there is a sudden stop; all are silent and the long rows of priests are still. Then the Bible is read.[86]

Another dance in Aksum, Ethiopia, is performed on the church porch:

Priests and deacons grouped themselves in a ring, in the center of which were two pairs or two groups of three, each group closely followed by a deacon, who beat a drum. They then performed a sort of counter dance, resembling a quadrille.[87]

Symbolic movements of the mass. Religious dancing has also survived—though submerged—in the mass. The mass has definite movements and postures for the participants and especially for those who have the active service of transferring books, candles, censers, offering plates, and other articles of the ritual. These symbolic movements are close to a disciplined dance. In fact, Robert Hugh Benson, who became a Roman Catholic priest, wrote of the mass in *Papers of a Pariah,* "It is no less than a sacred dance."

Also, in the play *Father Malachy's Miracle* by Brian Doherty, Father Malachy remarks, "But after all, holy mass is really a dance, isn't it? A beautiful dance upon the altar to Gregorian music!" Jacques Maritain, sensitive to the beauty of the disciplined movement in the mass, writes, "There is nothing more beautiful than a high mass, a dance before the ark in slow motion." [88] Even *A Catholic Dictionary* has this statement in its discussion on dancing: "Some of the movements . . . in sacred ceremonies (for example, celebrant, deacon, and subdeacon at high mass) are in the nature of a formal dance." [89]

133

A TIME TO DANCE

In order to explain the mass to young people, Ronald Knox repeatedly refers to parts of the mass as "dance" in his book *The Mass in Slow Motion*. He brings out the complete involvement of the whole person in the mass:

The introit gives you a nice sense of squaring your shoulders. . . . After the introit we go on to the real grovel. The point is that whenever you approach almighty God in prayer you ought to be bowled over, at the very start, by the thought of his unutterable greatness. . . . So, we say *Kyrie eleison*. . . . And the thing we use to cheer us up is the *Gloria in excelsis*. . . . And when, at the beginning of the gloria, the priest parts his hands and raises them and then brings them together again with that sort of scooping motion, he is (as it were) inviting our Lord to become incarnate and come down to earth. . . .

In saying, "The Lord be with you," the priest puts his hands apart, . . . and then brings them together again. . . . I think there's an obvious . . . significance about this latest movement in the dance. The priest, as he swirls around to make us feel at home, wants to include all of us in his greeting, and so he stretches his hands out wide. . . . All through this bit, the movements of the dance are rather complicated. . . . You have come to mass to worship God, and that means worshiping God with your whole being, not just bits of it.

[*Oremus*] generally means something is going to happen; a new movement in the dance is just going to begin. . . . The mass is a continuous action.

The offertory [offering of bread and wine to God] is really rather an important part of the mass, and all the more so because in a sense, this is where you come on. . . . Those two small boys in red cassocks . . . represent the congregation. In theory, you are all erowding on to the sanctuary, turning the priest's solitary dance into a tumultuous round dance. . . .

The mass is like that . . . ; we alternate continually between rushing to God with the consciousness of our needs, and then being driven back into a kind of shamefaced, tongue-tied humility

134

by the thought of God's majesty and our insignificance. Those are the two motifs that constantly cross and recross, making up the pattern of the dance for us. . . .

We unite, in offering the mass, not only with all faithful Christians all over the world, but with the dead too. . . . With these, the pure in heart, we will form one single ring about the eternal altar. . . .

Sursum corda; lift up your hearts! . . . It means take a deep breath and let your whole self go *out* to God [in the spirit of gratitude]. . . . The characteristic attitude of Christian people in worshiping their God is thankfulness. . . .

Don't encourage the choir to make the *Sanctus* into a great hullabaloo. . . . The whole dance of the mass depends, just here, on getting that effect of sudden calm, sudden dying away of noise. . . . [It's as if the priest says,] "*Sssh!* I've seen it! The glory of God, that fills earth and heaven, shining in front of me. Take off your shoes, and let's go in very quietly, on tiptoe." . . .

I have represented the mass to you . . . as a kind of ritual dance.[90]

Here is a present-day explanation of the mass as a ritual dance which has lasted throughout the centuries of the Christian church.

6

In

the Twentieth

Century

Leaders in Christian churches, both Protestant and Roman Catholic, are now pioneering in the use of symbolic dance. These leaders are aware of the traditions from the past nineteen centuries but are starting afresh with new symbolic ways for the liturgy in the twentieth century. They are influenced by meaningful works of contemporary professional dancers but are venturing into creative areas of communication through movements that go beyond modern-dance technique.

PROFESSIONAL DANCERS

Although professional dance is mainly theater-centered rather than worship-oriented, it contributes to man's spiritual searchings when its works speak about the worth of man and the mystery of the Creator. Worship is not limited to a church sanctuary; it can be expressed in a theater when there is meaningful involvement by the observers as well as by the dancers. Just as members of church singing choirs appreciate operas, so leaders and members of symbolic dance choirs in churches appreciate the skilled works of professional dancers.

Ruth St. Denis and Ted Shawn. Ruth St. Denis was the first American pioneer in religious dance, starting in 1912, as a result of her interest in oriental religions. One of her well-known contributions to the art is "The Masque of Mary," which she presented in 1939 at Riverside Church in New York City. In a dedicated and mystical way she has danced "the measures of the eternal music."

Ted Shawn was training for the Methodist ministry when he happened to see Ruth St. Denis dance. He was struck by her art and its spiritual projection, and shifted his interest to dance as a profession. In 1914 he and Miss St. Denis formed the Denishawn School to train future dance leaders.

Ted Shawn presented the first dancing in Protestant Christian worship in 1917 in the Interdenominational Church in San Francisco. He danced the opening prayer, the Doxology, a Gloria, an anthem, the Twenty-third Psalm, and a sermon—"Ye Shall Know the Truth." It was a daring experiment, but it was well received by the critics and the large congregation. Soon afterward Mr. Shawn went on tour with his Dance Church Service to some thirty cities, meeting with opposition in only two.

In 1933 Ted Shawn organized the first company of men dancers. They included in their programs "Jesu, Joy of

138

Man's Desiring," "O Brother Sun" (St. Francis), and "Job."

"A Sense of Ministry" was the title of *Time* magazine's report (August 21, 1964) of the fiftieth anniversary for Ruth St. Denis and Ted Shawn in their profession. Their vision and energy have been a true ministry as they have inspired, trained, and encouraged both dancers and church groups in the potentials of religious dance.

Erika Thimey. Erika Thimey of Washington, D.C., came from the Mary Wigman School in Germany in 1931 and contributed to the start of religious dance, mainly in Unitarian churches. In Chicago in 1932, in New York in 1933, and in Boston in 1934, she was active with church presentations. Inspired by Miss Thimey's creative work in 1935, Douglas Horton asserted, "All the arts ought to be brought back into the church, including the interpretive religious dances as instruments . . . of worship."

Doris Humphrey. Doris Humphrey had a rare ability to present humanity in symphonic-like dance design. Winthrop Palmer characterized her as possessing "a grave and passionate search for truth, a faith in justice, an infinite pity for humankind." "Inquest" was one of her compelling dances of social concern. Edwin Denby referred to it as an "eloquent sermon." Indeed, this "sermon" has remained clearly in my memory for many years, whereas verbal sermons heard in that same period have been forgotten.

Martha Graham. Because of the deep significance of Martha Graham's dances, serious-minded people have become more interested in contemporary dance for its value in penetrating revelation, rather than for entertainment alone.

A TIME TO DANCE

Many of Martha Graham's dances reflect upon or probe into religious concerns. "Appalachian Spring" projects various religious moods. The program notes provide the description:

Part and parcel of our lives is that moment of Pennsylvania spring when there was a "garden eastward in Eden." Spring was celebrated by a man and a woman building a house with joy and love and prayer; by a revivalist and his followers in their expression of exaltation; by a pioneering woman with her dreams of the promised land.

When Martha Graham toured in the Pacific as part of "The Arts and Exchange of Persons," Walter Terry made this comment in his report:

It was brought up in our discussion that there had been a famous editorial in an anti-American newspaper in Indonesia which commented that America was a land of dollars, gadgets, and bombs, and that only when Martha Graham danced there, under State Department auspices, did Indonesia discover that America had a soul.[1]

There should be more encouragement of groups that express the "soul" of people in America, for communication

through dance is more readily understood than verbal translations of ideas.

José Limon. José Limon's disciplined strength, in his dancing and in his choreography, has had a powerful effect upon the importance of men in religious dance. In the "Visitation" there is the dynamic masculine Gabriel and the solid masculine Joseph. "The Traitor" shows the powerful crosscurrents of the men who are Jesus' disciples. In his choreography and dancing of Kodaly's *Missa Brevis* (1963) José Limon has presented a balance of humility and grandeur. In "There Is a Time" [2] (from Ecclesiastes) he has used the circling design as a symbol of both time and timelessness. The great opposites of life are portrayed as experienced in time, yet ever recurring.

Other distinctive dancers. Innumerable religious contributions are being made by modern dancers. Among them are: Hanya Holm's "Parable," Anna Sokolow's "Song of a Semite," Pearl Lang's "Song of Deborah," Pearl Primus' "Sometimes I Feel like a Motherless Child," Sophie Maslow's "From the Book of Ruth," Helen Tamiris' "Five Spirituals," Noami Aleh-Leaf's "Sabbath Ritual," Eugene Lo-

141

ring's "These Three—And Then There Were Four,"
Pauline Koner's "Farewell."

Jean Erdman, dancer and choreographer, has written
that the modern dancer gains "an immense amplification of
spiritual experience" because the individual loses himself
in this art. "Today when the cult of the self-defensive ego,
the self-expressive . . . individual has cut us all off from
the unnamed immensity within us, dance again can serve
as a mystery of transfiguration." [3]

There are many teachers of dance in universities, where
the dance groups contribute to chapel services. Martha
Cornick, Patricia Jewitt, Forrest Coggan, and Mary Jane
Wolbers have given leadership in colleges and in summer
conferences.

What a wealth of creative works these professional
dancers have presented in the twentieth century! Just as
the wake of a boat widens and spreads out, so an ever-in-
creasing number of new dancers are adding breadth to the
exploration of the religious potentials in contemporary
dance.

LEADERS IN PROTESTANT CHRISTIAN CHURCHES

The earliest leaders in the use of symbolic movement in
Protestant Christian churches were influenced partly by

Ruth St. Denis, Ted Shawn, and Erika Thimey and partly by their own individual searchings to find new and meaningful ways to express acts of worship. Each one started without any knowledge of the creative ventures of the other church leaders.

William Norman Guthrie. William Norman Guthrie, the rector of St. Mark's-in-the-Bouwerie, an Episcopal church in New York City, was the first to sponsor religious dance. Between 1925 and 1938 he presented vesper services in which eurythmic rituals (as he entitled them) were presented by both professional dancers and members of the congregation. About seven vesper programs were given each year. "The Ritual Office and Dance of the Della Robbia Annunciation to the Blessed Virgin" was presented as an annual event. The choreography was by Bird Larsen, a talented and spiritual professional dancer; the music was Wolf Ferrari's *Vita Nuova.* The program had a disciplined dignity and graceful flow of movement. Although the bishop of the diocese attacked the presentation, the fact that he had never seen it lessened the force of his negative attitude. In a letter to the bishop, Dr. Guthrie described the eurythmic ritual:

> The lighting was so arranged as to give a sense of impersonality. . . . What followed did not resemble in the least a dance, but the performance of the mass raised to an ideal perfection. . . . Here it was the virgin who was glorified by assisting angels. The movements of the participants suggested . . . Fra Angelico angels.

William Norman Guthrie's interest in the arts of poetry and music supplied him with a wide field of subjects. His daughter, Phoebe Anna, planned the choreography for most of the numbers in the later years. The "Hymn of Jesus" from the Acts of John was presented to the music of Gustav Holst's cantata. In a program note Dr. Guthrie wrote: "Our friends and critics are invited to seek for the beauty of holiness or for the holiness of beauty, and bear witness that the age of creative, living devotion is not necessarily gone from the church."

Robert A. Storer. In 1937 Robert A. Storer wrote his B.D. thesis on "The Dance in Sacred Ritual." Later, as pastor of the Unitarian church in Dorchester, Massachusetts, he pioneered with his church youth in presenting "A Christmas Masque" in choreographic form. Now, from the Unitarian church in Winchester, Massachusetts, after twenty-five years of steady work with his motion choirs and with the training of leadership in the art of symbolic movement, he writes:

For the most part we will continue to be amateur dancers in the church, making use of movement to enrich what we are trying to "say," but not dancing—really dancing. . . . What we do in the sanctuary we regard as an element in a worship service, and not a concert number.

144

Margaret Fisk Taylor. Margaret Palmer Fisk[4] directed the youth of the South Shore Community Church in Chicago in Christmas, Easter, and special vesper services with simplified modern dance (1935-38). In Hanover, New Hampshire (1938-50), she worked with youth and adults, high school girls and college men in annual choir festivals. Reporting on a choir festival in *The Dartmouth,* a student wrote: "This group [the Hanover Rhythmic Choir] has brought a little bit of culture into an otherwise miserable period of world history. . . . Further, this work has done something to restore to the church some sort of meaningful ritual." In the years since she left Hanover, Margaret Fisk (Taylor) has been active with adults, youth, and children throughout the country—teaching in seminaries, summer college sessions, and conferences; leading workshops; writing books[5] and articles; producing filmstrips; and participating in television programs.[6]

Evelyn Broadbent. Since 1940 Evelyn Broadbent, wife of a United Church of Christ minister, has been active in this field. Her master's thesis (1943) at the Chicago Theological Seminary was on "The Use of Dance in Religious

145

Education." First in Easton, Connecticut, then in Brockton, Massachusetts, and Syracuse, New York, and now in Concord, New Hampshire, she has brought gifted and trained leadership to motion choirs for church people. In 1963 she sponsored "A Service of Evening Worship in Sacred Dance" for the annual meeting of the New Hampshire Conference of the United Church of Christ. There were nine choirs (sixty participants) in this service of worship.

Increased activity. During the last twenty-five years many excellent leaders have become active in their churches and in church conferences across the country; such as, Helen Gray, Virginia Lucke, Nels Andersen, Martha Hammond, Joan Johnson, Louise Mattlage, Patricia Sonen, Shirley Fritz, and Constance Fisher. And now there are more than one hundred skilled, dedicated leaders of church groups.

The Sacred Dance Guild was formed in New England in 1955 to stimulate dance as a religious art and to provide a means of communication for directors of dance choirs in that region. Most of the directors were from Congregational, Unitarian, or Methodist churches. In recent years the Sacred Dance Guild has widened its membership to persons of all faiths throughout the United States. Its newsletter, which is published three times a year, announces workshops, festivals, and the varied activities of its members. It also offers suggestions on resource material [7] and includes articles on creative approaches and on the underlying philosophies of this contemporary art. The editor urges the members to speak out on their convictions and to respond to the convictions of others. There is stimulation through the divergent views. The membership now includes persons from Baptist, Brethren, Episcopal, Evan-

146

gelical United Brethren, Hebrew, Lutheran, Methodist, Presbyterian, Roman Catholic, Unitarian-Universalist, United Church of Christ, and other religious groups.

Following a sequence of letters of opposing views from members of the Sacred Dance Guild, this note by the editor of the newsletter appeared in the January, 1963, issue:

> The Sacred Dance Guild members are a genuine, confusing, but healthy mixture of professionally trained dancers, those who have had a little dance training, and church workers who experiment on the level of a religious folk art. We cannot expect exact clarification or uniform agreement even in a "stated" purpose. We are in a burst of new creative explorations with tremendous potentials for speaking to our time through inspired, disciplined, improvised, planned movement! And I believe God may appreciate this variety of expression!

ROMAN CATHOLIC CONTRIBUTIONS

The Roman Catholic Church encourages contemporary artists to interpret Christianity in ways that are meaningful today. Although creative movement choirs have rarely participated in the sanctuary during the mass, occasionally interpreting choirs have done so in France, Holland, Germany, India, England, and the United States.

An early use of creative movement was witnessed in the Sacred Heart Church in Pittsburgh, Pennsylvania, in 1932. Hilary Pepler, a Dominican tertiary from England, was visiting in Pittsburgh. After only a few rehearsals he was able to present a medieval portrayal of the stations of the cross with a group of children of grade-school age. He had chosen the children at random, for he believed that no high talent was necessary to be able to portray the mystery. Not a word was spoken by the children as they progressed from one station to the next. At each station of the cross the children expressed the mood of pathos or agony that was communicated. It was a moving experience for the congregation.

There has been repeated use of creative dance at Grailville, in Loveland, Ohio, since 1948 when Lydia Mulders of Holland introduced symbolic movement. Since then there has been continuous exploration in this art form among the young women in the Grail Movement. In 1963, in Grailville, dancers of various races from around the world performed a scene from *New Born Again,* a folk drama which has been filmed. It combines spirituals, folk verse, and dance to portray the story of man's redemption. At the Grail Center in Brooklyn, New York, on Passion Sunday in 1959, the young women presented *The Cosmic Tree.* This included an interpretation of Psalm 50; "Love Is Come Again"; and the symbolic portrayal of the flowering cross in heaven, to the music of *Vexilia Regis.*

A motion choir interpreted the mass in the auditorium of Wichita University in 1953. Father Celestine and two altar boys were on an elevated level. Seven dancers (two men and five women), on the stage level, interpreted the begging for mercy in the Kyrie, the rush of glad tidings in the Gloria, the Credo with symbolic designs, on through the sequence of the mass.

In the fall of 1961 at Marygrove College in Detroit, Michigan, three dancer-reciters, directed by Sara Lee Stademan, presented "Teresa of Avila" and "The Litany of Divine Praises." Teresa was interpreted by Mary L. Robb as a robust and forthright saint. Mrs. Stademan

149

turned to Greek drama in using the other two dancers
as figures in St. Teresa's memory. The two responded as
a small Greek chorus with dance and speech. "The Litany
of Divine Praises" was based on an early litany set against
the musical background of Varese's *Poem Electronique.*

Benedictine monks have harmonized words, music, and
dance into a "balletorio" (a ballet-oratorio). Fathers Alban
and Mathias, who are members of the Order of St. Bene-
dict at St. Procopius Abbey in Lisle, Illinois, worked together for two years with Frederick Toenniges, choir
director of the Evangelical United Brethren church in Na-
perville, Illinois, formerly of the Detroit Symphony Orchestra. Two hundred and fifty students, townspeople,
singers, dancers, and musicians were involved in this new
work, *A Light in Darkness,* which included the creation
of the world, the birth of Christ, the crucifixion, and
the resurrection. It centered, according to the creative
monks, in "the emotions of the people involved in the
situations of the Bible." This was first presented in the
fall of 1961.

The Glenmary Sisters of Christ the King Convent,
Fayetteville, Ohio, presented *Alleluia—A Child of Promise*
in 1964. In this biblical-choral drama by Eusebia Hunkins,
a sacred dance choir interpreted major portions. (This
identical selection was interpreted by a Jewish group from
the Hillel Foundation at Ohio University—an example
of the free adaptation of art by any religious group.)

"The Catholic Hour" on NBC-TV (produced in cooperation with the National Council of Catholic Men)
gave a series on "Art and the People." On January 20,
1963, there was a program on "Movement and the Dance,"

presented by the Rev. William F. Lynch, S.J. It emphasized that dance can bring a sense of relatedness between people: "With the help of our bodies we can achieve an inner harmony and move no longer alone but in unison with other human beings. Thus, moving together, and knowing we do, we form true friendships and the order of love." The narrator expressed the idea that professional artists should become more closely involved with plain people:

We propose that you come out among us in America and either find us or help us find ourselves. You must stop patronizing us. You must send your real artists out among us and we will work together. At first we will be shy and difficult, but the human greatness will come out of us and we will teach you what real movement and style is.

There can be an exciting mixture of people (folk) and dancers mutually learning from each other and developing a tremendous source for communication between man and man.

INDIGENOUS CHRISTIAN WORKS

Roman Catholic. There has been a general policy in the Roman Catholic Church to welcome the indigenous art forms and the artists of every country where missionaries of the church are at work. The people who express ideas through group rhythms and symbolic gestures have been encouraged to express Christian ideas through their own ways of movement and design.

Norman O'Connor, C.S.P., writing on "New Song unto the Lord" in *Saturday Review,* said: "Ultimately, the music of the liturgy should create prayer. This is its aim.

My prayer may be an intense act of mind and emotion that may reflect itself in a dance or a recitation or in a creed. This is the test." [8]

The importance of response was expressed in the presentation of a choreographed mass on May 26, 1967, in the new Cathedral of Christ the King, in Liverpool, England. This choreographed mass consisted of a series of simple modern dances presenting the rite visually in images set to Cavalli's *Missa Concertata*. It was based on the response of the congregation which was expressed in choreographed images of worship, suffering, pain, glory, and hope. The altar served as the visual focus of the whole work.

At the 1965 International Eucharistic Congress, in Bombay, India, part of the liturgy was interpreted through the medium of Indian dance forms. Father George Proksche, S.V.D., who encouraged this creative work, wrote:

This close relation between the dance and religion in Hindu thought should inspire Christians. One wonders if the dance might not be a vehicle of conveying Christian religious thought. India is accustomed to seeing religion expressed . . . in exquisite poetry that is always chanted and, whenever possible, accompanied by a harmonious movement of body, hands, and face. The Hindu is so used to seeing religion expressed in this graceful way that the Western presentation of it seems unnatural and incomprehensible. . . . Why should we not follow the Hindus' example and try to present the glory of Christ's good tidings within the context of Indian culture.[9]

In describing his creative work for the Marian Congress in Bombay a few years earlier, he wrote:

We created a series of dances showing scenes of man in paradise, the temptation of the devil, the fall into sin, the prophecy of a Redeemer and the coming of our Lady as the bearer of the Savior. They all followed the traditional music and dance forms of India; there was a cast of 300 dancers and 1,000 singers. Thirty thousand people, among them Christians, Hindus, Muslims, Parsees, and Jews, saw the dancers, and the impression made on them by this depiction of Christian thought in Indian cultural forms was tremendous. Later, we were asked to go to the Eucharistic Congress in Munich to perform a sacred dance before the Blessed Sacrament. At the steps of the altar, just before the *Tantum Ergo,* with 300,-000 people watching, an Indian dance of praise, thanksgiving, and adoration was performed by twelve Catholic girls accompanied by six Hindu singers and musicians. Impressive presentations like these encouraged us to continue to experiment in introducing India's rich culture at least into the paraliturgical rites of the church.[10]

Protestant Christian. Protestant missionaries in the past have introduced little symbolic movement in their work. Some of them made it clear that the Christianity they revealed was a religion with no movements for the worshiper except to bow the head or to kneel. In South Africa, a Christian convert was referred to as "he who has given up dancing."

It is encouraging to know that a few Protestant Christian workers have been able to appreciate some of the native religious dances and have adapted them to the service of the Christian church. After visiting churches in South India, John Foster, professor of church history in Birmingham, England, wrote:

We saw dancing in the courtyard of the church. . . . The leader tells a Bible story, such as the deliverance from Egypt. The dancers form two concentric circles moving in opposite directions. Each dancer has a stick and as he passes each member of the other ring he taps his stick. Feet beat rhythmically, sticks tap to the same rhythm and through it all come the chanted words of the story with a refrain (like "The Lord came down to Egypt") oft repeated in which all the dancers join.[11]

In the June, 1947, issue of *Pilgrim Youth Magazine,* there was a picture of Indian girls in symbolic poses, with the caption: "These graceful Christian dancers in India are called *Kurmis.*"

A motion picture film, *The Cross in Togoland,* described the work of the Evangelical and Reformed Church (now United Church of Christ) in Africa. In it a religious dance-drama of the story of David was performed showing how native religious dance patterns have become effective Christian channels for expression.

From Angola, Africa, Harriet Summerville wrote in 1958, "I helped the children present the Christmas story in scripture, song, and rhythmic movement. They express as much by body as by mouth." She told of working with thirteen girls—teaching them some movements and then encouraging them to make adaptations that seemed "more natural to them."

In Kuala Lumpur, Malaya, Mrs. Lee Kong Beng has created symbolic interpretations with a group of young women who are teachers and secretaries. In 1961, Mrs. Gunnar Teilmann wrote of a rhythmic choir in the Wesley Methodist Church in Singapore, "The rhythmic choir has wonderful possibilities with our Malayan people."

Joyce Peel of the Diocese of Madras, Church of South India, wrote in 1962:

Two years ago I produced a whole program of psalms interpreted by dance and drama and choral speech for a service of preparation for Christmas. We started with the Lord's Prayer, followed by your [the author's] version of Psalm 27, which I took from your filmstrip; then my own version of Psalm 23. . . . We did it in the church and the atmosphere was most reverent. It was all very revolutionary. Those taking part were Anglo-Indians and they very much enjoyed it. . . . We did the Lord's Prayer kneeling all the time so that there would be less disturbance. The old people like to join in but getting up is a distracting effort for them, and I wanted it to be real prayer. . . . "As we forgive others" was shown by the "Peace" gesture—the folding of the neighbor's hand in our own—which we use in the communion service of the Church of South India to represent our fellowship; taken originally from the Syrian Church. For "hallowed be thy name" we had the Indian form of full prostration. [In this form] I have taught the Lord's Prayer to children in the villages and to Hindus and to illiterates. They learn the prayer with gestures. My colleague, who is doing religious drama in North India, and I have written a book, *Drama in the Church*. In it I wrote a chapter on "Interpreting the Psalms Through Movement." . . . This is a great field of missionary work for the future, so please encourage your mission boards to take up this work.

The important matter would seem to be to waken those who go out to the various countries to the possibilities of the art of interpretive movement and to the use of the indigenous dance forms as a base for further creative work. The basic ideas and the possibilities should be presented to world ministry workers, but the creative work should be done with the people who would use their own symbolic movements.

Such encouragement for each country or area to work out its own way of worship or symbolic movements was given in a statement by an English clergyman:

I would not agree more about the need to Africanize our worship. . . . In some sectarian groups the worship is always purely African—African music, African singing, African dancing. There is one I know in Northern Rhodesia where, as the two church elders stand holding the collection plate, the people come out of their seats and dance up to put their money in. That would liven up a lot of our services! Africans express themselves through dancing. It is one of their great art forms. . . . But—it is a very big "but"—we Europeans cannot Africanize; it has to be the African Christian leaders themselves who do the job.[12]

Toyohiko Kagawa, who inspired many Japanese to become Christians, wrote in 1950 to a friend:

In Japan we have a ritual dance as the one in honor of the Bon. A rhythmical play brought together with a muscular movement rouses one to a great joy of life. The men of old danced before God from gratefulness. Today a higher religion has become separate from dancing. But I do not always think that religion for children must be separate from dancing. I think it needful that life's rejoicing be represented in the form of dancing. As both Miriam and David did, children may freely dance in a religious sense. And with the children their parents, sisters, and brothers may well dance a folk dance to their hymns.

This opening to the use of religious dance for children is being explored by Japanese Christians working with children.

A presentation in traditional Japanese dance forms of the personal testimony of Mrs. Futaba Hanayagi captured on film is one of the newest developments in the use of sacred dance by the Christian church. The film, entitled *It Is Well with My Soul,* was recently produced by the Audio Visual Activities Commission of the National Christian Council of Japan. "The performance is an attempt by a talented Japanese artist to share the joy of her faith with others through the unique medium of traditional dance form."[13] The Japanese artist has a sacred dance choir assist her in this creative work. The film was shown at the Art and Mass Communication Seminar sponsored by the East Asia Christian Conference in Hong Kong in 1964.

At the same conference, Mrs. Shona McTavish, who has been active in religious dance in New Zealand, trained a group of Chinese girls in an interpretation. "This is perhaps the first time," it was reported, "that a regional conference sponsored by the Protestant Christian church in Asia, Africa, or Latin America has given major consideration to the dance as a means of Christian worship."[14]

A "Festival of Christian Arts" was held in the Philippines in 1963. Ralph Milton discussed, in a report on this festival, the need for the arts in worship. He included dance, which he described in this way:

Dance can most properly be defined as interpretative movement. Movement with meaning. Movement performed to convey an impression, a significance frequently symbolic. . . . The discussion was sparked by an interesting and challenging interpretative dance by four college girls (of Silliman University).[15]

157

This dance was based on Psalm 23. At the festival, also, a film was shown of a Thai classical dance interpretation of John 3:16.

Christians throughout the world use the ecumenical language of symbolic movement to interpret Christ to their people today.

EXPRESSIVE MOVEMENT IN RELATED FIELDS

Television. There are many television programs in which professional dancers perform religious numbers. They are excellent performances and absorbing for the observer. Increasing skill is being developed in the use of the special medium of TV, allowing for fade-ins for action and fade-outs after a mood has been communicated. This was particularly apparent in the telecast of *L'Enfance du Christ* by Berlioz, with the John Butler dance group, a symphony orchestra, and a choir.

Commenting on the *Ballet of Job,* Ann Bartzel, television reviewer for *Dance Magazine* wrote in the June, 1964, issue: "The piety of Job, the happy togetherness of his children, Job's physical agony were clear enough. . . . However, the real issues of the book of Job—man's destiny, his relation to God, ethical concepts involved—were not even hinted at." Such evaluation is appreciated and points to the need of more interrelating of ideas between religious leaders and dancers so that the dancers may be more aware of the depth of meaning in the subjects they plan to present in dance form.

There should also be opportunities for nonprofessional symbolic movement choirs to be televised during a devotional service. The members of these choirs are not "performing dancers," but are as integral a part of the worship service as acolytes or members of the church singing choirs. It could be a severe limitation in communicating the Christian faith if members of a symbolic movement choir were replaced by professional dancers when a service is televised. There should be opportunities for both the professional performing artists and the nonprofessional worshiping interpreters. Their purposes make them different even if they both use movement.

CHRISTIAN EDUCATION OF CHILDREN

Leaders in Christian education in many denominations are cognizant of the value of the total involvement of the child through creative dramatic movement, and therefore provide a deeper memory groove for learning. *Time for Wonder* and *Time for Discovery* by Margaret Fisk Taylor, *Using Movement Creatively in Religious Education* by Pat Sonen, and eight filmstrips[16] are available for Christian education workers. *The International Journal of Religious Education* and magazines published by the Methodists, Unitarians, Presbyterians, Lutherans, and by the United Church of Christ, carry articles encouraging this creative art.

Lord of the Dance: An Approach to Religious Education by Violet R. Bruce and Joan D. Tooke of England is now available in the United States. The authors have made many valuable suggestions. They contend that "in dance and dance-drama children can at least come to know that religion is a living thing; it is here and now." [17] One chapter deals with Old Testament material that can be developed through dance-drama. A depth of theological implications is presented in the descriptions of motivations for dances based

159

on New Testament themes. A stimulating chapter on "Problems of Present-day Life" brings out the dynamic potentials for group movement relating to conflicts of different generations, race relations, automation, leisure time, war and peace, and then ends with a section on *Joie de Vivre*:

Life and sheer living is full of joys. . . .

The Christian religion resounds with notes and tones of joy, abounds with promises of hopefulness. . . . Spiritual joy and life may have a deeper and different dimension but they are related at every point to ordinary things and happenings. . . .

Dance may be a joyous expression of moving together, in unison, or with joined hands in a circle or in a line, as in folk dance which is itself so often a happy culmination of work done, expression of the feeling that the world is a good place. Joyous movement is radiating, it communicates with the world, it seeks to include all that is around, it is infectious, bringing alive the dull and slothful. . . .

Joyous dancing, explosive, gay or gently happy, peaceful, appreciative or expressing simple pleasure, must for all groups be part of the religious education expressed through dance and dance-drama. There is a tendency for more creative work to be often dark and tense. The world is full of tension and tragedy and it is good that we can express it. There is fine dramatic quality here and to use it brings understanding and sympathy, but the world is also full of joy, so let us dance sometimes joyously.[18]

In this world of tribulation, Christians need to recall the clear words of Christ to "be of good cheer" (John 16:33) and need to remember the Old Testament writing which declares that besides a time when one mourns there is certainly "a time to dance" (Eccles. 3:4) with joy.

Therapy. There is increasing use of simple movement as therapy for those who are mentally or emotionally disturbed, for the delinquent, the retarded, the disabled, and the handicapped. In all these fields leaders are exploring and finding release for the disturbed,[19] involvement for the delinquent, enjoyment for the retarded, and assistance for the handicapped.[20] The churches are concerned with all persons (in or out of their churches) who find themselves separated from others through some handicap of mind or body. There are more and more workshops for training in simplified dance for the deaf,[21] blind, retarded, and disturbed. Church people can get suggestions at these workshops and then adapt the ideas through their own creative efforts. Leaders in the field of movement therapy will accomplish more by their own outgoing *acceptance* of each individual and their *encouragement* of some improvised movement by the handicapped than by technical training alone.

The dance therapist is not teaching dance in order to develop a performing artist, but is using her technical skills and her personal creativity and spontaneity to enable people to become more aware of themselves on a human, realistic level. In order for her to dare to work in terms of basic communication in body action, she must have resources sufficiently rich so that she can dare to free herself from specific technical forms. . . . We are a word-centered culture, and we sometimes ignore the things we are saying directly with our body action. Patients are more aware of expressions of feeling from other people than many of us are. The leader must realize that there can be nothing artificial about her responses. . . . Obviously, the dance therapist must have special training in order to make use of so vital and direct a means of relating. . . . But no amount of training will be of any use unless there is within the person the sensitivity, creative spontaneity, and freedom of expression essential to the process of dance therapy.[22]

CHURCHES ENCOURAGE PARTICIPATION

The churches are speaking today through people and to people by means of expressive movement. They encourage the children, youth, and adults to explore and participate in creative movement in Christian education, summer conferences, festivals, and worship services.

The National Council of Churches, which sponsored a "Consultation on the Dance" in 1960, has been encouraging more emphasis on all the arts, including dance. In 1963 the Department of the Arts of the National Council of Churches included this concern in its proposals: "The department should have commissions dealing with particular artistic media (for example, worship, drama, literature, music, architecture, the dance, popular arts)." Among the emphases of the department was: "the encouragement of creative activity in the realm of the arts on the part of the churches themselves, including local congregations."

What is the local congregation but the people in the church? The future of this devotional art will be influenced not by the artists alone, nor by the leaders in the National Council of Churches alone, nor by the people in the congregations alone. The future will bring a meaningful growth in this art as there is intercommunication and mutual respect because of a common purpose—to express a living response to God's presence in the world today.

O Lord, our heavenly Father, we offer and present unto thee ourselves, our souls and bodies, to be a reasonable, holy, and living sacrifice unto thee. Take us as we are and make us more fit for thy service. . . . Use us as thou wilt, to the glory of thy holy name and the good of our fellowmen; through Jesus Christ our Lord. Amen.[23]

Appendix 1
Resources

Mary Jane Wolbers has compiled a list of resources entitled "Resources in Sacred Dance." It is the most complete list of books, periodical literature, unpublished manuscripts, audiovisual materials, and other suggested resources on sacred dance as an art form and the use of sacred dance in worship and religious education. The list is available from Mrs. Charles Wolbers, 111 South Green Street, East Stroudsburg, Pa. Supplements appear annually in the newsletter of the Sacred Dance Guild.

The New York Public Library has a compiling of all materials on sacred dance and a file of newsletters of the Sacred Dance Guild.

VISUAL AIDS

The following visual aids present works of Margaret Fisk Taylor and her symbolic movement groups.

Filmstrips. The color filmstrips listed below are available for purchase through Dr. Ruth Lister, 126 Garden Avenue, Grove City, Pa. 16127.

A TIME TO DANCE

> *Jesus Walked This Lonesome Valley*
> *Relating to Others, a Lonely One*
> *The Story of Ruth*
> *Psalm 27*

Motion pictures (16 mm.). The following motion pictures are available for rental from Dr. Lister.

> *Worship the Lord* (Rhythmic Choir of Hanover, N.H.), 20 minutes, color
> *Worship Through Symbolic Movement* (TV film of youth of Westminster Presbyterian Church, Dayton, Ohio), 25 minutes, b & w
> *Appalachian Mass* (TV film of Symbolic Movement Choir of Athens, Ohio), 10 minutes, b & w

Appendix 2

The Lord's Prayer— Antiphonal Reading

(Italics indicate words to be emphasized.)

OUR FATHER We *center* our thoughts upon thee, Father of us all.

WHO *art* IN HEAVEN We sense thy *infinite* existence.

Hallowed BE THY NAME We are *humble* in thy presence.

THY KINGDOM *come* We seek the *revelation* of thy will.

THY WILL BE *done* May thy will be done through *each one* of us.

ON *earth* AS IT *is* IN HEAVEN Thy will is one on earth and in heaven.

Give US THIS DAY We ask for the *gift* of daily sustenance.

Our DAILY BREAD And we would share with *others*.

AND *forgive* US OUR DEBTS *Forgive* us our failures and selfish actions.

AS *we* FORGIVE OUR DEBTORS As we forgive *others* with outgoing love.

AND LEAD US   *not* INTO TEMPTATION   *Help* us when we feel the pull of sin away from thy will.

BUT *deliver* US   FROM EVIL   We *turn* to thee in humility, but also with hope.

FOR THINE IS THE *kingdom*   Unity and *exaltation* are here!

AND THE *power*   Thy power *streams* forth!

AND THE *glory*   Thy *glory* is ever with us!

FOREVER   The *eternal* is even in *this* moment.

AMEN   We *ask* this to be so—in *our* lives and for *thy* sake. *Amen.*

Note: Each symbolic movement choir should adjust the descriptive phrases to relate to the emphases of ideas that are being expressed.

Appendix 3
Guidelines

The following principles have been worked out by Joan S. Johnson and the members of her worship choir to clarify the purpose and the discipline of the group. Each member keeps a copy of the guidelines as a reminder.

1. I will dedicate myself to the purpose of glorifying God and not myself.

2. I know the day and time we regularly rehearse and therefore I will plan my activities so I can be present regularly and on time.

3. I know that attendance at rehearsals and services is important, that I am important in the group to carry out my individual part. Therefore, perfect or near-perfect attendance is an absolute must. I will think twice before asking to be excused from a rehearsal and will never, except in an emergency, ask to be excused from a service.

4. I know that rehearsals are held in order to work on interpretations. Therefore, I will come prepared to work and do it for the full time without fooling around or filling in with talk, homework, or other activity.

5. Each of us can be a check on the other members by reminding one another of our responsibility whenever talking or inattention starts. I can set an example.

6. My attitude at rehearsals will be reverent since our work is to worship.

7. I realize we are working toward a common goal—that we should all pull together toward this goal.

8. I will accept the discipline required to make our choir good.

9. I agree that persons who come into the choir should belong for a trial period in which they learn about its work and then decide if they are willing to give the time and effort necessary; otherwise they should drop out.

10. I will make devotions a more important part of choir. When individually assigned to give devotions, I will create my interpretation of a hymn. I will remember humbly to ask help for myself and for the choir from God.

11. When I have questions about what we are doing or suggestions and ideas, I will bring them up for discussion so that the interpretations will truly be the work of the total group—members of the choir and the director.

12. I know that the choir director is here to help me individually, that I can talk with the director on any subject on which I need guidance.

13. I will be responsible for my robe and be willing to pay for loss and mistreatment of it.

14. I will always act and speak reverently when practicing in the chancel.

Notes

Introduction

1. A *liturgical* art is one in which people take an active part in public services of worship.

Chapter 1   The Art of Symbolic Movement

1. See Margaret Palmer Fisk, *Look Up and Live* (St. Paul: Macalester Park Publishing Co., 1953), chap. 2.
2. Martha Graham, "A Modern Dancer's Primer for Action," *Dance: A Basic Educational Technique*, ed. Frederick R. Rogers (New York: Macmillan, 1941), pp. 181 f.
3. John Martin, *Introduction to the Dance* (Brooklyn, N.Y.: Dance Horizons, 1965), p. 53.
4. Paul Tillich, *Theology of Culture*, ed. Robert C. Kimball (New York: Oxford University Press, 1959), p. 56.
5. Paul Tillich, *Symbolism in Religion and Literature*, ed. Rollo May (New York: Braziller, 1960), p. 77.
6. Ira Progoff, *The Symbolic and the Real* (New York: Julian Press, 1963), p. 214.
7. Evelyn Underhill, *Worship* (Harper Torchbooks; New York: Harper & Bros., 1957), p. 23.
8. Written to the author by Fred Eastman, former professor of biography and drama, Chicago Theological Seminary.
9. See Harvey Cox, "The Gospel and Postliterate Man," *The Christian Century*, Nov. 25, 1964.

Chapter 2   Starting a Symbolic Movement Choir

1. Jerome Bruner, *On Knowing: Essays for the Left Hand* (Cambridge, Mass.: Harvard University Press, 1962), p. 20.
2. Von Ogden Vogt, *Art and Religion* (Boston: Beacon Press, 1948), p. 78.
3. Jacques Maritain, *Art and Scholasticism*, trans. J. F. Scanlon (New York: Charles Scribner's Sons, 1930), pp. 54 f.
4. Patricia Jewitt, "Dance," *Guide for Drama Workshops in the Church*, ed. Amy Goodhue Loomis (New York: National Council of the Churches of Christ in the U.S.A., 1964), pp. 24, 22. Used by permission.
5. Violet R. Bruce and Joan D. Tooke, *Lord of the Dance: An Approach to Religious Education* (New York and Oxford: Pergamon Press, 1966), pp. 4 f.
6. Maritain, *op. cit.*, p. 55.
7. The prostrate position may be used, for example, with the hymn "All hail the power of Jesus' name, let angels prostrate fall!"
8. Robert Horan, "The Recent Theater of Martha Graham," *Chronicles of the American Dance*, ed. Paul Magriel (New York: Henry Holt & Co., 1948), p. 254. Copyright 1948 by Dance Index. Used by permission of Holt, Rinehart and Winston, Inc., Publishers.
9. José Limon, *7 Arts*, ed. Fernando Puma (New York: Doubleday, 1953), p. 62.
10. Based on a workshop problem presented by Mary Anthony at the Sacred Dance Guild Workshop in New York City in 1961.
11. Limon, *op. cit.*, p. 62.
12. Ruth H. Rayton, "A Time for Sacred Dance," *Children's Religion*, June, 1964, p. 15.
13. Betty Meredith-Jones in her statement before the Consultation on the Dance (1960), sponsored by the National Council of Churches, 475 Riverside Drive, New York, N.Y. 10027.
14. Rayton, *op. cit.*, pp. 14 f.

Chapter 3 Using Movement in Festive Services

1. Described in Margaret Fisk Taylor, *Time for Discovery* (Philadelphia: United Church Press, 1964), pp. 27 ff.
2. See Appendix 1, "Filmstrips," pp. 163 f.
3. William Norman Guthrie, *Offices of Mystical Religion* (Century, 1927), pp. xxix, 406.
4. This choral music is published by Marks Music Corporation, 136 W. 52d Street, New York, N.Y.
5. See Appendix 2, "The Lord's Prayer—Antiphonal Reading," pp. 165 f.
6. Described in Taylor, *op. cit.*, pp. 67-70.
7. Nathan A. Scott, Jr., "Art and the Renewal of Human Sensibility in Mass Society," *Christian Faith and the Contemporary Arts*, ed. Finley Eversole (Nashville, Tenn.: Abingdon Press, 1962), p. 28.

Chapter 4 Dramatizing Religious Ideas

1. John A. T. Robinson, *Honest to God* (Philadelphia: Westminster Press, 1963), p. 87. Published in the U.S.A. by the Westminster Press, 1963. © SCM Press Limited, 1963. Used by permission.
2. Doris Humphrey, *The Art of Making Dances*, ed. Barbara Pollack (New York: Holt, Rinehart and Winston, 1962), p. 112. Copyright © 1959 by Charles F. Woodford and Barbara Pollack.
3. *Ibid.*
4. *Ibid.*, p. 113.
5. For a fuller description, see Margaret Fisk Taylor, *Time for Discovery* (Philadelphia: United Church Press, 1964), pp. 50-53.
6. See Appendix 1, "Filmstrips" *Relating to Others, a Lonely One*, pp. 163 f.
7. See *Life* magazine, March 8, 1948, pp. 99 f., 102.
8. See Appendix 1, "Filmstrips," *The Story of Ruth*, pp. 163 f.
9. See Appendix 1, "Filmstrips," *Psalm 27*, pp. 163 f.
10. See Appendix 2, "The Lord's Prayer—Antiphonal Reading," pp. 165 f.

A TIME TO DANCE

Chapter 5   The History of Symbolic Movement

1. W. O. E. Oesterly, *The Sacred Dance* (New York: Macmillan, 1923).
2. G. R. S. Mead, *The Sacred Dance in Christendom*, "The Quest Reprint Series," No. 2 (London: John M. Watkins, Sept., 1926), p. 65.
3. Hipp. Ref. v. 10.
4. *Didache* xi. 11.
5. Clement of Alexandria *Stromata* V. iv. 19.
6. Clement of Alexandria *Exhortation to the Heathen* xii. 119 f.
7. Origen *De Prec.* vii. 5.
8. Gregory Thaumaturgus *Four Sermons* i.
9. Gregory Thaumaturgus *Hom.* iv. (*De Christi Bapt.*).
10. Eusebius *DVC*, xi.
11. Eusebius *VC*, II, xix.
12. *Hom.* vi. (*In Eccles.*) 4.
13. Gregory of Nazianzus *Oration Against Julian* ii. 171.
14. See C. H. Brömel, *Fest-Tantze der ersten Christen* (Jena, 1701).
15. Basil *Epistle* xl.
16. B. Aubé, *Homélie inédite en append. à Polyeucte dans l'histoire* (Paris, 1882), p. 79.
17. Ambrose *On Repentance* ii. 6:42.
18. Ambrose *Commentary on the Gospel of St. Luke* vi.
19. Ambrose *Speech* xlii.
20. Chrysostom *Hom.* i. (*In illud. vidi Dom.*) 1.
21. Chrysostom *On the Resurrection of Lazarus* i.
22. Chrysostom *Proaem in Pss.*
23. Augustine *Speech* cccxi.
24. Theodoret *Graecarum Affectionum Curatio* xi.
25. Theodoret *In. Vis. Dan.* iii. 57.
26. Arg. (*Int. Jonae Proph.*).
27. *Eucharistic Prayers from the Ancient Liturgies*, chosen and arranged by Evelyn Underhill (London: Longmans, Green & Co., 1939), p. 55.
28. Simon de la Rosa y Lopez, *Los Seises de la Cathedral de Sevilla* (Seville, 1904).
29. Claes Lagergren, *Mitt livs minnen*, III (Stockholm, 1924);

172

NOTES

paraphrased in E. Louis Backman, *Religious Dances in the Christian Church and in Popular Medicine,* trans. E. Classen (London: Allen & Unwin, 1952), pp. 77 f.
30. *Analecta Hymnica* 2, 62 (Leipzig, 1890-1906).
31. *Ibid.,* 1, 207.
32. *Ibid.,* 53, 97.
33. *Planctus* of Cividale del Fruili. Cividale, Reale Museo Archeologico. Cividalenso Saec. xiv, foll. 74 ff.
34. See Renée Foatelli, *Les Danses Religieuses dans le Christianisme* (Paris: Éditions Spes, 1947), p. 95.
35. Bonaventura *Dieta Salutis (Aureus Libellus).*
36. Honorius *Gemma Animae* ("On Dancing").
37. Quoted in Backman, *op. cit.,* p. 66.
38. Mead, *op. cit.,* p. 99 n.
39. T. H. Poole, "Labyrinth," *The Catholic Encyclopedia,* Vol. IV (New York: Encyclopedia Press, 1907-22).
40. K. Bartsch, *Mittelniederdeutsche Osterlieder* (1880), p. 49.
41. *Ibid.*
42. E. Jacobs, *Rosengarten im deutschen Lied, Land, und Brauch* (Halle, 1897).
43. *Analecta Hymnica, op. cit.,* 16, 72.
44. *Ibid.,* 1, 137.
45. *Ibid.,* 20, 178.
46. *Ibid.,* 55, 69.
47. "The Dance of Death." See Florence Warren, *The Dance of Death* (London: Oxford University Press, 1931), p. 60.
48. Quoted in Foatelli, *op. cit.,* pp. 63 ff.
49. Lincoln Kirstein, *Dance* (New York: G. P. Putnam's Sons, 1935), pp. 85 f.
50. Dante *Divine Comedy* ("Paradise") VII.
51. *Ibid.,* XXIV. Italics added.
52. Kirstein, *op. cit.,* pp. 112 f.
53. Otto Kinkeldy, "A Jewish Dancing Master of the Renaissance: Guglielmo Ebreo," *A. S. Friendus Memorial Volume.* See Kirstein, *op. cit.,* pp. 117 f.
54. "The Last Judgment" in the Monastery of St. Mark in Florence, Italy.
55. Ethel Urlin, *Dancing, Ancient and Modern* (New York: Appleton & Co., 1914), p. 44.
56. In the museum of Santa Maria dei Fiore in Florence.

57. Roland Bainton, *The Martin Luther Christmas Book* (Philadelphia: Westminster Press, 1948), p. 76. Used by permission of Fortress Press.
58. William Dunbar (Scottish Text Soc., 1507), II, 116, 119.
59. Kirstein, *op. cit.*, p. 146.
60. Thoinot Arbeau, *Orchesography*, trans. Cyril Beaumont (London: Beaumont, 1925), p. 19. Used by permission.
61. Quoted in "Oratorio," *Grove's Dictionary of Music and Musicians,* ed. Eric Blom, Vol. VI (5th ed; New York: St. Martin's Press, 1954; London: Macmillan & Co., Ltd.).
62. Rites referred to in an anonymous letter to the *Mercure de France,* September, 1742. Translated from the Latin by Mead, *op. cit.*, p. 250.
63. Mead, *op. cit.*, p. 258.
64. *Ibid.*, p. 253.
65. Ménestrier, *Des Ballet Anciens et Modernes* (Paris, 1682).
66. Paraphrased in Backman, *op. cit.*, p. 37.
67. A pelota (or *pilota*) was slightly larger than a tennis ball.
68. See *The Oxford Book of Carols* (London: Oxford University Press, 1964), No. 71.
69. Johannes Boemus, *Omnium Gentium Mores, Leges et Ritus* (1520), fol. 58 b.
70. C. de Coussemaker, *Chants populaires des Flamands de France* (Gland, 1856).
71. Urlin, *op. cit.*, p. 48.
72. C. M. Kaufmann, *Handbuch der Altchristlichen Epigraphik* (Freiburg, 1917), p. 199.
73. Winfred Rhoades, "When Grief Stabs the Heart," *Advance,* Aug., 1949.
74. Backman, *op. cit.*, pp. 159 f.
75. See *Collections,* X (2d Series; Boston: Massachusetts Historical Society, 1823), pp. 183 f.
76. Published in Boston in 1688.
77. Backman, *op. cit.*, p. 100.
78. Edward D. Andrews, *The Gift to Be Simple: Songs, Dances, and Rituals of the American Shakers* (Locust Valley, N.Y.: J. J. Augustin, Publisher, 1940), p. 110.
79. *Ibid.*, p. 136.
80. Edward D. Andrews, "The Dance in Shaker Ritual," *Chronicles of the American Dance,* ed. Paul Magriel (New York:

Henry Holt & Co., 1948), p. 5. Copyright 1948 by Dance Index. Used by permission of Holt, Rinehart and Winston, Inc., Publishers.

81. Andrews, *The Gift to Be Simple, op. cit.,* p. 17.
82. George Meredith, *Poems.* (New York: Charles Scribner's Sons, 1905), p. 414.
83. Andrews, *The Gift to Be Simple, op. cit.,* p. 71.
84. Used by permission of Sydney Carter. See *Sing Round the Year,* songs selected by Donald Swann (New York: David White Co., 1966); or see *Risk: New Hymns for a New Day,* Vol. XI (New York: World Council of Churches, 1966), No. 3.
85. See Backman, *op. cit.,* pp. 116-21.
86. C. F. Rey, *The Real Abyssinia* (London), p. 190.
87. Backman, *op. cit.,* p. 93.
88. Jacques Maritain, *Art and Scholasticism,* trans. J. F. Scanlon (New York: Charles Scribner's Sons, 1930), p. 56.
89. *A Catholic Dictionary,* ed. Donald Attwater (3d ed.; New York: Macmillan, 1962).
90. Ronald Knox, *The Mass in Slow Motion* (New York: Sheed & Ward, 1948), *passim.* Copyright 1948 by Sheed & Ward, Inc. Used by permission.

Chapter 6   In the Twentieth Century

1. Walter Terry, "Panel on Exchange in Dance," a report on "The Arts and Exchange of Persons," Oct. 4-5, 1956, at the Institute of International Education, New York, N.Y.
2. "There Is a Time" (No. 2171) is featured by the National Education Television Film Service; it can be secured through Indiana University, Bloomington, Ind.
3. Jean Erdman, "The Dance as Nonverbal Poetical Image," *Dance Observer,* May, 1949.
4. Since 1957, Margaret Fisk *Taylor.*
5. *The Art of the Rhythmic Choir* (New York: Harper & Bros., 1950); *Look Up and Live* (St. Paul: Macalester Park Publishing Co., 1953); *Time for Wonder* (Philadelphia: United Church Press, 1961); *Time for Discovery* (Philadelphia: United Church Press, 1964).

6. See the filmstrips and motion pictures listed in Appendix 1, pp. 163 f.

7. *Resource Materials,* edited by Mary Jane Wolbers, 111 S. Green Street, East Stroudsburg, Pa.

8. Norman O'Conner, C.S.P., "New Song unto the Lord," *Saturday Review,* April 10, 1965.

9. George Proksche, "The Sacred Dance: A Great Classical Art Is Adapted to the Liturgy," *Jubilee,* Nov., 1964.

10. *Ibid.*

11. John Foster, *Then and Now: The Historic Church and the Younger Churches* (New York: Harper & Bros., 1942), p. 102.

12. J. S. Kingsnorth, "The Changing Role of Missionary Societies in Africa," *Journal of the Royal Society of Arts* (London), Feb., 1963.

13. *Sight-Sound,* Dec., 1964.

14. *Ibid.*

15. Ralph Milton, "Philippine Churches Sponsor a Festival of Arts," *The Silliman Christian Leader.* Reprinted in *Sight-Sound,* Dec., 1964.

16. Available from Dr. Ruth Lister, 126 Garden Avenue, Grove City, Pa. 16127.

17. Violet R. Bruce and Joan D. Tooke, *Lord of the Dance: An Approach to Religious Education* (New York and Oxford: Pergamon Press, 1966), p. 1.

18. *Ibid.,* pp. 97-100.

19. For suggestions on release from tension, see Margaret Palmer Fisk, *Look Up and Live, op. cit.,* pp. 33-44; and Margaret Fisk Taylor, *Time for Discovery, op. cit.,* pp. 32-35.

20. See Leda Canino, "The World Opens," *Dance Magazine,* Oct., 1964.

21. *Beyond Silence,* a dance film based on sign language, presented at the National Cathedral in Washington, D.C., by deaf students of Gallaudet College, Washington, D.C. Available at Memorial Library, Gallaudet College, Washington, D.C.

22. Marian Chace, "Dance Alone Is Not Enough," *Dance Magazine,* July, 1964.

23. Prayer from *The Book of Worship for Church and Home* (Nashville, Tenn.: Board of Publication of the Methodist Church, 1965), p. 108.

Selected
Bibliography

Amberg, George. *Art in Modern Ballet*. New York: Pantheon Books, 1946.

Andrews, Edward D. *The Gift to Be Simple: Songs, Dances, and Rituals of the American Shakers*. Locust Valley, N.Y.: J. J. Augustin, Publisher, 1940. Republished in 1962 by Dover Publications, Inc.

Arbeau, Thoinot. *Orchesography*. Translated by Cyril Beaumont. London: Beaumont, 1925. Republished in 1966 by Dance Horizons, Inc.

Armitage, Merle. *Dance Memoranda*. New York: Duell, Sloan & Pierce, 1947.

Arvey, Verna. *Choreographic Music: Music for the Dance*. New York: E. P. Dutton & Co., 1941.

Attwater, Donald (ed.). *A Catholic Dictionary* (3d ed.). New York: Macmillan, 1962.

Backman, E. Louis. *Religious Dances in the Christian Church and in Popular Medicine*. Translated by E. Classen. London: Allen & Unwin, 1952.

Bainton, Roland. *The Martin Luther Christmas Book*. Philadelphia: Westminster Press, 1948.

Blom, Eric (ed.). *Grove's Dictionary of Music and Musicians* (5th ed.). 9 vols. New York: St. Martin's Press, 1954.

Bruce, Violet R., and Tooke, Joan D. *Lord of the Dance: An Approach to Religious Education*. New York: Pergamon Press, 1966.

Bruner, Jerome S. *On Knowing: Essays for the Left Hand*. Cambridge, Mass.: Harvard University Press, 1962.

The Catholic Encyclopedia. 15 vols. New York: Encyclopedia Press, 1907-22.

Denby, Edwin. *Looking at the Dance.* New York: Pellegrini & Cudahy, 1949.

Dickinson, Edward. *Music in the History of the Western Church.* New York: Charles Scribner's Sons, 1902.

Duncan, Isadora. *My Life.* Garden City, N.Y.: Garden City Publishing Co., 1927.

Ellis, Havelock. *The Dance of Life.* Boston: Houghton Mifflin Co., 1923.

Eversole, Finley (ed.). *Christian Faith and the Contemporary Arts.* Nashville, Tenn.: Abingdon Press, 1962.

Ferm, Vergilius (ed.). *Encyclopedia of Religion.* New York: Philosophical Library, Inc., 1945.

Fisk, Margaret Palmer. *Look Up and Live.* St. Paul: Macalester Park Publishing Co., 1953.

Foatelli, Renée. *Les Danses Religieuses dans le Christianisme.* Paris: Éditions Spes, 1947.

Foster, John. *Then and Now: The Historic Church and the Younger Churches.* New York: Harper & Bros., 1942.

Guthrie, William Norman. *Offices of Mystical Religion.* Century, 1927.

Hastings, James (ed.). *Encyclopedia of Religion and Ethics* (2d ed.). 13 vols. New York: Charles Scribner's Sons, 1951.

H'Doubler, Margaret. *Dance: A Creative Art Experience* (2d ed.). Madison, Wis.: University of Wisconsin Press, 1962.

Humphrey, Doris. *The Art of Making Dances,* ed. Barbara Pollack. New York: Grove Press, 1962.

Johnson, F. Ernest (ed.). *Religious Symbolism.* New York: Harper & Bros., 1954.

Kinney, Troy and Margaret. *The Dance: Its Place in Art and Life* (rev. ed.). Frederick A. Stokes Co., 1914.

Kirstein, Lincoln. *Dance: A Short History of Classic Theatrical Dancing.* New York: G. P. Putnam's Sons, 1935.

Knox, Ronald. *The Mass in Slow Motion.* New York: Sheed & Ward, 1948.

Lloyd, Margaret. *The Borzoi Book of Modern Dance.* New York: Knopf, 1929.

Loomis, Amy Goodhue (ed.). *Guide for Drama Workshops in the Church.* New York: National Council of Churches, 1964.

SELECTED BIBLIOGRAPHY

Magriel, Paul (ed.). *Chronicles of the American Dance*. New York: Henry Holt & Co., 1948.

Maritain, Jacques. *Art and Scholasticism*. Translated by J. F. Scanlon. New York: Charles Scribner's Sons, 1930.

Martin, John. *America Dancing: The Background and Personalities of the Modern Dance*. New York: Dodge, 1936.

—————. *Introduction to the Dance*. Brooklyn, N.Y.: Dance Horizons, 1965.

May, Rollo (ed.). *Symbolism in Religion and Literature*. New York: Braziller, 1960.

Mead, G. R. S. *The Sacred Dance in Christendom* ("Quest Reprint Series," No. 2.). London: John M. Watkins, Sept., 1926.

Mettler, Barbara. *Materials of Dance as a Creative Art Activity*. Tucson, Ariz.: Mettler Studios, 1960.

Morgan, Barbara. *Martha Graham: Sixteen Dances in Photographs*. New York: Duell, Sloan & Pierce, 1941.

Oesterly, W. O. E. *The Sacred Dance: A Study in Comparative Folklore*. New York: Macmillan, 1923.

Palmer, Mrs. Winthrop. *Theatrical Dancing in America: The Development of the Ballet from 1900*. Bernard Ackerman, 1945.

Perugini, Mark Edward. *A Pageant of the Dance and Ballet*. London: Jarrolds, 1947.

Phillips, William. *Carols*. New York: E. P. Dutton & Co., 1921.

Progoff, Ira. *The Symbolic and the Real: A New Psychological Approach to the Fuller Experience of Personal Existence*. New York: Julian Press, 1963.

Puma, Fernando (ed.). *7 Arts*. New York: Doubleday, 1953.

Ritter, Richard H. *The Arts of the Church*. Boston: Pilgrim Press, 1947.

Roberts, Grace. *The Borzoi Book of Ballets*. New York: Knopf, 1946.

Robinson, John A. T. *Honest to God*. Philadelphia: Westminster Press, 1963.

Rogers, Frederick R. (ed.). *Dance: A Basic Educational Technique*. New York: Macmillan, 1941.

Sachs, Curt. *The World History of the Dance*. New York: W. W. Norton & Co., 1957.

St. Denis, Ruth. *An Unfinished Life: An Autobiography*. New York: Harper & Bros., 1939.

Seldon, Elizabeth. *The Dancer's Quest: Essays on the Aesthetic of the Contemporary Dance.* Berkeley, Calif.: University of California Press, 1935.

Shawn, Ted. *The American Ballet.* New York: Henry Holt & Co., 1926.

———. *Dance We Must.* Printing & Binding Co., 1940.

———. *Gods Who Dance.* New York: E. P. Dutton & Co., 1929.

Taylor, Margaret Fisk. *Time for Discovery.* Philadelphia: United Church Press, 1964.

———. *Time for Wonder.* Philadelphia: United Church Press, 1961.

Thompson, Betty Lynd. *Fundamentals of Rhythm and Dance.* New York: A. S. Barnes & Co., 1933.

Tillich, Paul. *Theology of Culture,* ed. Robert C. Kimball. New York: Oxford University Press, 1959.

Underhill, Evelyn (ed.). *Eucharistic Prayers from the Ancient Liturgies.* London: Longmans, Green & Co., 1939.

———. *Worship.* New York: Harper & Bros., 1957.

Urlin, Ethel. *Dancing, Ancient and Modern.* New York: Appleton & Co., 1914.

Vogt, Von Ogden. *Art and Religion.* Boston: Beacon Press, 1948.

Vuiller, Gaston. *The History of Dancing.* New York: Appleton & Co., 1898.

Warren, Florence. *The Dance of Death.* London: Oxford University Press, 1931.

Young, Karl. *The Drama of the Medieval Church.* Oxford: Clarendon Press, 1933.

This book may be kept

FOURTEEN DAYS

A fine will be charged for each day the book
is kept over time.

MAR 4			
OCT 21 1985			
MAR 28 2002			
SEP 21 2005			